"Pa...
it'...
— The New York Post

"Brilliantly funny."
— Pittsburgh Post-Gazette

"Fiendishly Funny."
— San Francisco Chronicle

"The funniest thing you'll read this year."
— NPR's Marketplace

KASPER HAUSER'S

EARN YOUR
MBA
ON THE TOILET

UNLEASH
UNLIMITED POWER AND WEALTH
FROM YOUR BATHROOM

Original artwork by James Yamasaki, Jayson Wynkoop, and Vince Bohner

TEN SPEED PRESS
Berkeley

CONTENTS

FOREWORD

BY ROB DELANEY

LOOK OVER THERE. See that palace on the hill? How did it get there? If you're an idiot, or a "poor," you probably guessed that someone built it. WRONG. Maybe you "built" your slanting hovel down by the railroad tracks, but a palace materializes fully formed due to the Power of Business. And that just so happens to be Lesson One of business school: "If you point at a hill, you can make a palace with your mind." I hope you wrote that down—or at least didn't cross it off the page after you read it, because there will be a test and that test is called Life, Terry.

You'll notice I've decided your name is Terry. Maybe that's not the name your parents gave you, but God damn it, it's your name now. I've made a decision, and that's business.

Business: it's as old as rocks and as elemental as fire. When you see a timeworn black-and-white photograph of a bearded man with his brow furrowed and his collar made of Dutch papyrus, chances are he's thinking about business. Is his business pleasure? Why, that's none of your . . . you guessed it: BUSI-NESS! See? Business can be fun too! Just ask President Mitt Romney. When you see him tilt that leonine head back and bark out a few staccato "HA! HA! HA!s" you can bet your gingham SARS mask he's having fun.

I'm not entirely certain why Kasper Hauser asked me to write the foreword to this book. Is it because I took the money my cousin earned from his childhood paper route and turned it into a dynamic media empire that makes CNN look like a ragged burlap sack of decomposing donkey meat? Is it because Barack Obama himself came to my yacht* in January of 2009 to beg me to save the global economy from collapse by leveraging my collection of Fabergé dog eggs against the Chinese yuan? Is it because I told Steve Jobs I'd mount a hostile takeover of Apple and sell it to the Saudis if he didn't figure out a way to fit my encyclopedic collection of Eagles bootlegs between my buttocks back in 1997? I'd have to guess that yes, all of those achievements are factors in Kasper Hauser asking me to write this foreword. Or maybe, like the rest of the world, they wanted to hear from the man Bill Gates himself called "a f#ck-ing monster," and Warren Buffet deemed "the Pol Pot of modern commerce." Yes, I've known my fair share of success! But the difference between me and the aforementioned novices is that I've always wanted more than my fair share. I've wanted your share and her share and his share too. And I've taken it, with the power of business, whose language I've mastered, for I am a Master of Business. If you read this book, you'll be a Master of Business as well. If you read it twice you'll be a Doctor of Business. Thrice, and you'll look Donald Trump in the eyes at the same time you f#ck him in the ass. How will you achieve that? Read on, Terry . . .

---

*The *S.S. Suede Resolve*, Grand Cayman Island

Join the 1 percent . . .
without leaving your toilet!

INTRODUCTION

WHAT ARE YOU *DOING* with your life? Not succeeding, that's what. And you're not alone . . .

Hundreds of billions of men and women say they wish they were doing more, earning more, or giving back more, getting the love they want, getting to yes, or getting the f#ck out of Dodge and starting to start their own start-up.

Are you sick of hoping for a better future? Of having people tell you to take some ownership of your career—to "shit or get off the pot"?

Now you can do both. The book you're holding in your hands will literally pump your potty time into a Brain-Xpanding Tragetunity™. The Kasper Hauser Toilet Training Series is a revolutionary new paper book–based system that literally converts shit into gold.

BUSINESS CAN BE ANYTHING YOU WANT!

Here's our value proposition: instead of reading the same old pee-splattered copy of *Thursdays with Bilbo* every morning on the can, how about using that time to get an Ivy League*–level education instead?

Here's the advantage of our system: unlike at a fancy private college, it doesn't take literally *forever* to go through one of our courses. Instead, you can complete an entire semester in about the time it takes to make a Belgian waffle.

Welcome to the New School, D-bag!

Earn Your MBA on the Toilet will allow you to Master the Business Arts from the comfort of your own toilet, or maybe your parent's toilet, tripling and in some cases doubling your potential income!

Written for the busy professional, the unemployed CEO, or the motivated alcoholic, this incredible course condenses thousands of hours of business wisdom—what we call Buswodmisness™—into a fun and terrifying crash course, chunked into eighteen baby "jam sessions."

---

* = "asterisk"

TALK ABOUT RETURN ON INVESTMENT!

Here's your first business lesson (and you haven't even officially started the course!): if you read only half of this book and then lose it, you will still have gotten $23,4567 of an MBA education at a 920 percent discount! That's cheaper than Greece!

And to those who say that this book cannot replace the valuable personal connections that you would have made at a "real" business school, we say, "yes ma'am!" That is a truly *crippling* weakness in our system.

> **If you get your MBA using this book, you will be profoundly and irrevocably stunted forever** in some respects. But in others, you will only be behind by a lot, and haven't people already said that you're a "lone wolf"; that they find you "hard to get to know" and "f#ckin' creepy"? YOU DON'T NEED THOSE PEOPLE. [Cut out this paragraph and tape it to your bicycle mirror!]

"But will I learn the same *material* here that I would at an actual business school?"

F#ck you, ya whiner.

The answer is: *why would you even ask that.* One hundred and ten percent yes it covers those things.

Each chapter covers a major topic taught by the world's most incredible business schools. Every paragraph has been gone over and gone over. Each subject has been pumped. We even have a chapter on vitamins.

HOW DOES THIS SOUND?

After eight trips to the toilet, you'll be able to hold your own with a finance professor* at a cocktail party.

After nine trips, you'll be qualified to work as a management consultant, and up and up it goes from there!

And at the end, when it's all over, you'll receive a certificate of completion that is definitely, literally an MBA degree on par with the big guys, basically.

So what are you waiting for? Wolf down some Grape Nuts® and a crappucino, and we'll see you in about an hour . . . at "Business School"!

But first: **Is an MBA the right degree for you? Read on . . .**

Hi, I'm Learning Dave, and I'll be your guide! Look for me to point out important tips and helpful concepts!

---

* The finance professor that you'll be able to hold your own with is named Terry Goodglenn. Not sure if he was in a motorcycle wreck or something, but you will definitely be blowin' this guy away.

CHAPTER 1

BEFORE YOU EMBARK:

WOULD A DEGREE IN METAL DETECTING BE BETTER FOR YOU?

AN MDA IS A DEGREE IN METAL DETECTING ADMINISTRATION. It's not a degree that's granted by any fancy institution—it's a gift you give to yourself. It means you have unlimited earning potential.

Having an MDA also means you're the guy in charge of the detector and no one can touch it because they'll break it because you have to know how to work the knobs and how far to hold it above the sand.

Q: How many beaches in the world? How much buried treasure on each beach?

A: Counting parks and deserts? Hard to say.

Just like with an MBA, metal detecting can send you home with your sack bulging with coins, but without the petty world of office politics.

Imagine a job where your office *was* the beach, where you could wear *your* pants, smoke a pipe on the job, and keep 110 percent of your earnings. How about masturbating on the clock? Under a full moon? Yes! No!

There are no limits, just like in skydiving.

Randy, gridding

You can do anything as a metal detector (in metal detecting, both the machine and the person are called "metal detectors").

According to Wikipedia, there are two techniques for using a metal detector for "beachcombing," which is the hobby of hunting for lost coins or jewelry on the beach: "gridding" is when you search in a pattern and "random searching" is when you walk around the beach in no particular pattern, hoping to cover more ground.

Does that sound incredible? If so, it may be time to bail on the MBA and go where the real money is—the buh-buh-buh-buh BEEEaach!

If you *would* rather pursue metal detecting, stop here and gently push the book between your legs into the water part of the toilet (the "bowl"). Give the book time to become water-logged and then flush.

Still serious about the MBA? If so, grab the top right corner of this page and carefully pull it toward your nose, then flick to the left!

WELCOME TO THE FIRST DAY OF THE LAST PART OF YOUR LIFE!

You just passed a MAJOR test. Metal detecting is for complete assh#les.

Welcome to the Beagle Patch. Let's get started. Record these phrases into a tape recorder (or iPhone):

I'm considerate.
I'm kind.
I'm weak.
I'm great.
I rule.
I'm cave-trash.
I'm a rat.
I'm beautiful.
I'm "CEO-grade."
I'm prepared.
I'm a liar.
I'm stupid.
I *am* a genius.
I *am* a minotaur.
I *am* a douchebag.
I *am* [say your name], *the most Business Black Belt of all time.*

LISTEN TO THE RECORDING AT ALL TIMES UNTIL YOU COMPLETE THE BOOK—and then listen to it only while you sleep, for the rest of your life. DO IT!

It's now time to learn!

CHAPTER 2

MICROECONOMICS AND MACROECONOMICS:
A TALE OF TWO ECONOMICSES

ECONOMICS IS THE WIDE-RANGING SCIENCE of how we behave in relation to the things that we want and need: candy bars, motorcycles, amphetamines, a real dolphin, etc. Let's take a deep dive:

> *A motherf#cker who we'll call "Steve"* decides to open up his own donut shop. He rents a space in a strip mall and borrows money from his Uncle Toby. Then he buys a DonutGlazer TK421™ and hires an assistant manager, Ray. Steve is ready to start making donuts—and a ton of money.*

Now, would Steve be trying to sell donuts if they literally grew on trees? No. Because of the **law of demand:** the more that there is of something, the lower the price that people will

---

* His real name is David Mary Michael James.

pay for it. If people could get donuts off of trees, brush the shit off, and eat them, they probably wouldn't pay cash for them. Except that fruit grows on trees, and it's *extremely* expensive! That's the part of the whole "grows on trees" analogy that's honestly f#cked. If money grew on trees, would it be cheaper than fruit?! WTF?

Anyways, Steve's plan isn't just to make donuts, but to focus on the donuts that people pay the most for: crullers (the braided round ones, not the little dick-shaped filled things). This is the **law of supply:** producers will increase production of things that sell for the most.

Steve's donut business had all the makings of a recipe for success. He didn't see any red flags. Nor did his friend Kyle. Whenever Steve told him about the donut shop he dreamed of opening, Kyle would giggle or give a "thumbs up" sign.

But within only a couple of weeks, Steve had filed for bankruptcy *and Kyle was gone.*

What happened?

Steve had misunderstood two of the most important "phenomenomics." First, **opportunity cost:** when someone chooses one thing, they give up something else. Because of the location of his shop, Steve's potential customers would have had to give up crack cocaine in order to buy his crullers. Crack is better than donuts. Hundreds of millions of times better.

Also, it turned out that Ray, his manager, was a mole for the Cambodian mafia, which has a monopoly on the donut business. Steve's shop would have provided **competition** to the Cambodians, nut-slapping the donut market. So Ray spray-painted the word "ปอเปี๊ยะทอด" on the hood of Steve's Miata. In Khmer, the official language of Cambodia, "ปอเปี๊ยะทอด" translates as "suck my Donald Dick, white choco-dile."*

---

* A grave insult among traditional peoples who consider Donald Duck to be a manifestation of Brhapîtli, The Water Dong.

Not all Cambodians are peace loving.

That made no sense, but even less so because Steve *wasn't* white—he was another kind: Korean, or Pacific Islander, the big guys. Samoan. But that didn't matter. The basic fact of economics was that Steve *wasn't* Cambodian.

And Kyle? Nobody knows where Kyle went. Maybe there is no lesson there.

Steve wanted it too much. But f#ck him, seriously. You . . . *you* can learn from Steve's mistakes. By mastering the concepts above (and continuing on with the next section), you can avoid the pitfalls that sunk Stevez Dream Cremez.*

Now let's take a deeper look at a fascinating, fascinating thing . . .

ECONOMICS OF DiFFeReNt siZeS!

Q: What is a *widget*?
A: It's a little thing about this big.

---

* And several other businesses that he ran into the ground: Steve once put real squirrel-monkey jockeys on racing dogs. Guess who got shot by a disgruntled gambler? Steve did, in the knee.

Through Steve's donut debacle (and they ended up killing him, by the way), you learned many of the key concepts of basic economics. The beautiful thing about the "dismal science" (as Mike Tyson famously dubbed the field) is that those basic concepts—supply, demand, competition, opportunity cost—operate at two very different levels: microeconomics and macroeconomics. Let's take a look . . .

MICROECONOMICS

Microeconomics can be described in a nutshell. That nutshell looks very small from our perspective, but from the vantage point of someone living inside of it, the walnut could feel as gigantic as the EnormoDome.

TELL ME MORE, SLUUUURP!

You see, economics functions on a personal scale, a small scale: even a tiny race of people (a people whose entire civilization

Microeconomics

could be wiped out by one errant clomp of a donkey's hoof) would respond to and go about satisfying their material wants and needs in a similar manner to us "ably sized" people.

ARE YOU FOLLOWING THIS?

For the sake of learning, say that you could shrink down to the size of one of these little shits. You might find that their economy would operate on a microscopic scale: they would have one-dollar bills with shrunken George W. Hobbit heads on them. They would have tiny "faerie" banks (with little safes made out of sardine cans) and interest rates that are barely visible to the naked eye. They would have a happy truce with cats and bats, unicorns and dumbledorns—all the magical denizens of this magical Walnut Land! And they would have infinitesimal gross national products, labor, markets, tariffs, even complex derivatives—exactly like us except way, *way* smaller.

But this is not just an analogy, a thought experiment. **This tiny race of people is real.**

They're called various things (Weezletums is one of the stupider names they have). The government has proof, but they won't release it. And while the Weezletums have plenty of upstanding li'l bankers and businessmen, they have many more than their share of wee robbers and rapists. In fact, one of the most notorious of these microscopic monsters, Old Mrs. Tumbletoyne, murdered the tooth faerie and kept him in a freezer the size of a mouse's teardrop. Still wanna be an economist?

We're not done.

MACROECONOMICS

On a hot, dusty afternoon, a vigilante named Pedro limps down the street of a hardscrabble town south of the border. We hear a crow, a radio, the buzz of a rattlesnake's tail.

Pedro

He stops at a worn-down cantina and pushes open the swinging doors. *"¡Puta!"* he says, resting a grimy hand on his revolver.

A few patrons inside are scattered about, sipping tequila and speaking in the local language, Spanish. And if they're discussing macroeconomics, you can bet they're using the term *"los grandes económicos."*

Why? Simple. *"Grande,"* in the words of our passionate but less fortunate neighbors to the south, is the word they have chosen to mean "big" . . .

And that's exactly what macroeconomics is: big.

Macroeconomics is the study of the behavior, the function, the structure, the performance—the workings, if you will—of the economy of the whole universe. Including the dark realms, *la materia oscura del* Big Bang!

When you imagine macroeconomics, picture in your mind "an enormous thing" *infinitely larger than a whale*—or even, some day in the future, the ability to land a woman on the moon and return her safely to Earth.*

Luckily there are only four terms in all of macroeconomics:

- Inflation
- Deflation
- Unemployment
- Income and Production

And thankfully, they are all so mind-clubbingly basic that they need not be defined here. (If you want to know more, Google them! As a business leader, you're going to encounter

---

*Macroeconomics can get that big, if you dare to dream. And that's what business is all about: *¡Sueños!*

Adam Smith believed that the economy was
guided by an invisible hand (above).

a lot of questions you don't know the answers to. You'll need to
turn to the Internet for instantaneous information. Start famil-
iarizing yourself with some search engines. Aside from Google,
there is Bing, Blekko, Volunia, Youdao, ChunkIt, Clutsy, Dog-
pile, Brainboost, Mobissimo and Yehey! [Philippines], just to
name a few. Also, Yahoo!, once the king of the web, was eating
shit at the time of publication, so hedge your bets by learning
about a backup portal.)

Hey Grrrl, you just finished the economics chapter! Fold,
wet, and wipe, and we'll see you later this afternoon!

In a PowerPoint presentation: what is between the slides?

POP QUIZ!

1. **Draw a line from the term on the left to the definition on the right that best defines the term:**

   Macroeconomics   "Big" economics

   Microeconomics   "Small" economics

   Example:

   Macroeconomics ────────────────▶ "Big" economics

   Microeconomics   "Small" economics

2. **In a _____ are _____.**

   A. Supply and demand
   B. Competition
   C. Inflationary economy, everyone has to carry everything around in wheelbarrows
   D. Can't wait to finish this book

3. **Milton Friedman**

   A. Was a ramblin' man.
   B. Was a hoochee-coochee man.
   C. Was a back-door man.
   D. Was a renowned econo-hobo.

4. **The following is an example of "opportunity cost":**

   A. An opossum gets his head stuck in a tennis ball can.
   B. A man finds that his cookie bags are rotten.
   C. An off-duty cop tries to clean a vacuum cleaner with another vacuum cleaner.
   D. A woman tries to return Ping-Pong balls after she's already played with them.

CHAPTER 3

FINANCE:
THE GAY "STAIRWAY TO HEAVEN"?

FINANCE IS SIMPLY THE STUDY OF MONEY, how it is used, and how it flows from one place to another. Through finance, we learn that we can *make* money do work *for* us, in the same way that Uncle Toby works for Nona and Peepaw.

To see how money works, we need to know a little about **business structure.**

Businesses are generally divided into **sole proprietorships, partnerships,** and **corporations.** Don't do the first one, the proprietorship one—especially if you operate hot air balloons—you'll end up on death row.

Finance is a very important topic! Wow. I never thought I'd be doin' this—wearin' a f#ckin' toilet on my head. Feels like I can't breathe.

So how do businesses make money? Mainly by offering *goods or services* or by *investing.* Let's learn by example: a company that sells snakes is offering "goods"; a company that offers to remove snakes from your toilet (or bidet) is offering a service; and a company that says, "You'll be blown away by how many snakes there will be when you retire" is dealing in investments.

Goods

Examples:

- ▹ Goods: We just told you! Snakes.
- ▹ Services: Hosing down a hot horse
- ▹ Investing: Stock market

NEED TO KNOW

OVERHEAD

When you finally pass this course and are sitting in a corner office somewhere, **overhead** will be part of your everyday life, a constant f#cking headache.* It is simply the sum total of all of a business's "costs of doing business":

Salary + Petty Cash + Business Lunches + Σ a (blabba + c) = D(i)do.

---

* If a manager is getting new or different headaches on a regular basis, that could mean a tumor. Remember: no tumors of the head are benign. Seek appropriate care: never try to remove your own brain tumor.

The math looks intimidating but it isn't. The "complicated" part of the equation, to use an example from above, simply means "snake (in toilet) + Σ a (box of snakes + kid's bed)."

Common examples of Overhead for a small business:
- grapefruit
- coffee filters
- snail mail
- nonpleasure books

Items that are not considered Overhead:
- hobbies

LEVERAGE

Leverage means simply that you made a big thing out of a little thing. An example from sea life would be a whale eating a huge whale: impossible, but *true*. They have them. They have the bones, so why not believe them?

CAPITAL BUDGETING

This is the process a company uses to decide which investments are worth it—which ways of using the company's money will bring the biggest gains in return (see "ROI" below). Probably not our place to suggest this but: why has no one done a huge art car with turntables, a hot tub, and a MONKEY DRIVER? F#ck. Maybe *we* should do it.

All right! Back now after a couple days. Thanks for waiting. Turns out the art car thing is—wow—illegal and dangerous. Hope the little guy finds his way back to 7-Eleven. God, that place *is* a dump. Chimpanese are ASSH#LES.

RETURN ON INVESTMENT (ROI)

This is the value that your company yields from an investment above and beyond what it put in.

Q: Can some ROIs be so big that they're "f#ckin' SICK"?

A: *Yes sir.*

So why not always pick the investment that yields the biggest return?

Because some are *riskier* than others . . .

RISK IS . . .

- ▶ How risky is it that something will happen?
- ▶ Is it "risky business"?
- ▶ Are you "taking too big of risks"?

One method to help estimate whether you and Emma (your business partner) are taking "too big of risks" is through **risk analysis.** This is a collection of theories, techniques, computations, and analytics that relieves anxiety and reduces liability by *predicting the future.*

Quantification of risk. Worth it?:
Jet Skiing   Y   N
Now have fun: Fill in your own dangerous thing! Do you have the balls?

_____

REALTIME LEARNING™

Let's say a clown was at a fair, and he said that he was selling pinecones out in the parking lot. You are a company. Do you go with him and invest in pinecones? NO. Because never go to somebody's car that you don't know. SOME OF BUSINESS IS JUST COMMON SENSE.

Sound reasonable enough? If so, you're ready to move on!

POP QUIZ!

1. **Which business entity is best for the given product or service?**

   A. A hippie lady who melts army men with a magnifying glass

   B. A dentist who doesn't use X-rays because he can "smell" bad teeth

   C. A company that buys rivers from naked people

   i. LLP
   ii. Doesn't matter
   iii. Corporation

2. **A boy with a hot dog wanders into the courtyard. It's 1828, Nuremburg. You decide to:**

   A. Try and talk to him (turn to page 128).

   B. Try and get the hot dog (turn to page 136).

   C. Sit down and put your hands on your head (close the book; put it in the toilet).

   D. Go back to sleep in your cave. You're a vampire (turn to page 21).

3. **Finance is the study of:**

   A. Monkeys

   B. Mondays

   C. Monets

   D. Money

4. **"Capital budgeting" is:**

   A. Always capitalized

   B. Sometimes capitalized

   C. A "worthwhile endeavor"

   D. Anyone have a koi tank for sale? Gotta get these things in water.

5. **A white man sells you a parrot for $500; you give it to your Meemaw but she can't find it now. Who's on the hook for this shit?**

   _____

   _____

CHAPTER 4

ACCOUNTING:
BLECCHHH!

ACCOUNTING IS HOW YOU KEEP TRACK OF IT ALL. It is the art of tabulating all aspects of your company's value and transactions. Using DynamicDefinitions™, we can learn while having a little fun!

We'll tell a simple business story and then define *every accounting term you'll ever need,* using the story as a reference. Here goes!

> **Donna** and Terry live on a houseboat with a diabetic cat named Bilbo. Terry also **has** diabetes, and one day discovers that he can use the cat's insulin without feeling bad. The vet charges Terry and Donna $8 per vial for Bilbo's insulin while Dr. Chan charges the couple $122 (cash, up front) for the same amount of human insulin. Terry goes to a "lifestyle" party one evening with the plan of eating some potato salad, hanging out, and having **sex** with a few new people in the group. He brings three vials of cat insulin just in case they have cupcakes. A white man with a beard named Peter asks what's in the vials.

"Liquid acid," says Terry, joking.

"I'll buy each vial for $100, three vials now and ten later," says Peter.

*"Okay, if you pay for half of them now," says Terry. Terry writes "IOU ten vials of humen [sic] LSD" on a condom wrapper and gives it to Peter. Terry only has sex **with** one more person so that he can leave the party early with the money and also so he can get back to the houseboat before his blood sugar gets too high. On the way home, he becomes ketoacidotic and T-bones a couple in a Thunderbird, totaling it. It's Donna with **Dr. Chan.***

GO BACK AND READ IT AGAIN.
GOOD. NOW CUT THE STORY OUT AND LAMINATE IT
SO YOU ALWAYS HAVE IT.

NOW WATCH THIS!

See how easy it makes these accounting concepts?

- **Accounts Payable.** The amount Terry owes for ten more vials of cat insulin, $80.
- **Accounts Receivable.** The amount Peter owes Terry for more liquid cat "acid," $650. Did Donna give Dr. Chan a hand job? Hmmm . . .
- **Assets.** Terry's houseboat, penis pump, Bilbo, and anything that Donna owns.
- **Cash Flow.** Pretty good. He got out of a sex party with $650! I think that's good.

- ▸ **Equity.** Everybody—black, white, Peter, Donna, Dr. Chan—everybody is equal. I don't care who it is.
- ▸ **Invoice.** The condom wrapper that Terry gives to Peter.
- ▸ **Liabilities.** Totaling the Thunderbird. Huge deal, sucks. Also, Terry slapped Donna and her glasses broke. That could be bad if Donna wants to go with Herb (Chan).
- ▸ **Statement.** What Terry tells his friend Deputy Dan before going back to the party to get laid.

Great! Let's take a learning journey!

THE BALANCE SHEET: KEEPING TRACK OF ALL THE ENDLESS BULLSHIT

We said that accounting was the art of tabulating all aspects of a business's value. Well, the result of all that tabulation—the statement, the report card, the snapshot at a given moment in time—of your company's financial status is called "the balance sheet." Without it, you're going to the electric chair.

 BETCHA DIDN'T KNOW

If you're doing business in another country, here is how you say "balance sheet": "shit-o de balanzia" (pronounced "SHEET-o day bal-AHN-zee-yah)

Now, there are two parts to a balance sheet: **assets** and **liabilities.** (Remember Terry's penis pump! Told you the story would help!)

CLOSER LOOK!

Let's see what the balance sheet "balances."

Assets are all of the resources a company possesses. Here are a few examples of some of the most common legitimate assets:

- ▶ Cash
- ▶ Real estate
- ▶ Coins
- ▶ Ripped-up, shredded cash or bent coins*
- ▶ Torn dollar bill taped back together**
- ▶ Bag of cash with "$" sign on it
- ▶ Wallet with money inside
- ▶ Uncashed paycheck (that you plan to cash)
- ▶ Coin collection
- ▶ Ferris wheel where each car is full of gold coins and the car has a trap door on the floor, and when it reaches the top, the door opens and coins rain down on the lucky carnival-goers

Possible assets:

- ▶ Gold-*plated* hamster cage (melted into coins of a made-up country)
- ▶ Indian corn

Not assets:

- ▶ Chocolate coins
- ▶ Any blown-out piece of shit

---

* Damaged or shredded money is *still an asset*. The trick is that it's worth less than unshredded money. But it's still worth something, even as hamster bedding. A classic rookie accounting mistake is putting torn dollars in the liability column. *It's not. It's an asset.*

** You have to play it cool when you hand the taped dollar bill to the cashier. Technically, it's not legit money, but once it leaves your hands and enters their hands, it's their problem, and you get to keep the Slurpee.

BETCHA DIDN'T KNOW

When an accountant records a business transaction,
this is called a *journal entry.* Check it out!

Journal Entry: Tuesday, April 5

Woke up early and tried on my new khakis from Old Navy.
Too tight today, even though they fit perfectly in the store.
I am like a supermagnet that attracts problems.

Now here are **liabilities.** These are what the business owes
in terms of money, goods, or services, including:

▶ Ripped-up or shredded cash
▶ IOUs
▶ Insurance payments that you owe (to the carnival-goers
   crushed by the Ferris CoinWheel Ride™)
▶ What it would cost to assassinate your biggest enemy
   (approx. 1 million dollars)

Possible liabilities:
▶ Bad luck
▶ No feet
▶ Having a learning dibisility

Taking this job was a bad choice.
I feel angry!

You can always get a balance sheet to "balance out" by erasing or adding a couple of zeros, ones, twos, fives, or sixes or eights, nines, threes, fours, or even sevens from one of the columns.

Got it all down? Good! So how do you actually fill out one of these things? Easy, just take the two lists (assets and liabilities) and carefully copy one thing in each line of the blank balance sheet that you got from Barbara, trying to keep your writing "within the lines" (you can steady your writing hand by resting your wooden one on top of it as you write) . . . and Viola! You're an accountant!

CLOSER LOOK!

STORING MONEY: SHOULD I USE A MONEYBAG?

If you love cartoons, you've probably seen robbers carrying bags with the "$" sign on them and you may have thought to yourself, "Should I put my money in one of those?"

Our recommendation is *not* to do that.

The dollar sign is a dead giveaway for robbers. And if the robbers steal your money, *they* will have the last laugh, and you'll be back to square one: an MBA graduate with a blown-out yogurt shop.

ZEN-O-NOMICS

A manager yells at a copyboy, and the copyboy says, "You wouldn't yell at me if you knew who I was."

"Who are you?" asks the man.

"Bilbo Baggins," says the boy (and he was).

Instead of a moneybag, take all of your one dollar bills to the bank, and trade them for a *single thousand dollar bill.* Keep this bill in a (waterproof) envelope in the top part of your toilet (the tank, *not* the bowl).

Q: Should I use a moneybag with the $ sign on it?
A. Yes
B. No

A: Depends. There are times when this is useful.

POP QUIZ!

1. **In the story, Terry and Donna love each other very, very much, but:**
   A. Bilbo's illness rips them apart
   B. Dr. Chan represents everything Terry could never give her: excitement in the form of he's a doctor
   C. Terry has continued to go to sex parties even though Donna quit in June
   D. All of the above

2. **Accounting is the process by which:**
   A. Companies take a hard look in the mirror
   B. Corporations begin to find themselves
   C. Companies explore their bodies
   D. Businesses look at their own butt h#le with their iPhone

3. **Socially, an accountant is:**
   A. Above you
   B. Below you
   C. Equal to you
   D. The lowest

4. **Adam Smith in *The Wealth of Nations* never discussed how much room a billion one dollar bills would take up. How much would it take up?**
   A. Forty storage containers
   B. The size would be gigantic
   C. Two fields
   D. Don't understand

CHAPTER 5

MARKETING THE MEDIEVAL WAY

Selling isn't all about sales.

—COUNT ARTHUR STRONG

THE TERM "MARKETING," when you think of its origins, helps you to understand it. In medieval times, the "market" was the place where vendors and buyers would meet. *It was also a place of whores.* And that definition stands to this day.

SCHOOL'S IN SESSION!

Let's keep the medieval theme going. Imagine you have an idea for an invention, a "widget" that peels off people's skin, and you want to sell it to the Spanish Inquisition. How will they know about your product unless you market it?

Whoa, hold on a second! Are you sure they even *want* to peel off people's skin?! If they don't, you're going to have a heck of a time selling them on the skin-peeler widget.

Q: Can a "widget" be a torture device?
A: *F#ck YES!*

You see, marketing isn't just about selling what you've got, it's about learning what the buying public ("the market") wants. This is called **inbound marketing**. In this case, your company must learn from the Spanish Inquisition what their needs are.

"*¡¿Como se dice 'Skin Peeler' en español?!*"

MARKETING QUESTIONNAIRE

What sorts of things would you like to know from the Spanish Inquisition? Let's say you sit down with Abiathnar de Lupa y Vallasco. Here are some "preguntas" you may want to "garganta" him:

- ▶ What are your skin-peeling needs?
- ▶ What problems have you encountered while skin-peeling/hurling babies at cattle/ripping people in half?
- ▶ Ow o wow ow! You're hurting me?
- ▶ What is your most embarrassing moment?
- ▶ Who in the Spanish Inquisition makes decisions about supplies for killing and torturing?
- ▶ Are you going to put my head or anus on a pole?

Your job of selling—**outbound marketing**—is much easier when you know that you're bringing a product to market that has demand. You *know* there is demand, because you asked the market directly, and they demanded it!

What now?! Time to maximize profits by:

1. Looking for "**adjacent markets**": Is there a Portuguese Inquisition? Maybe they want the skin-peeler widget too.

2. Convincing your customer to buy more products: "We also sell bird shit—not 'bird *shit*,' just different shit for your birds (cages, pellets, that little bone that they chew, etc.)."

3. Convincing your customer to buy a more expensive product (**upselling**): "We have a fine selection of gold-plated dog shit—not 'dog *shit*,' just shit for your dog that he'd like."

4. Convincing your customer to buy a more profitable product: "This isn't a potato peeler, trust me. It's for skin."

Through marketing, you communicate with the Inquisition, finding out how best to meet their needs by bringing products and services that help them meet their goals of gathering confessions and accusations, combating the Albigensian Heresy, and executing and torturing Muslims and crypto-Jews among *conversos* throughout the Iberian Peninsula. And doing it with a profit margin that keeps your company healthy and growing. *¡Vámanos!*

POP QUIZ!

1. Is "octopamine" a real thing?

A. Yes, it's like gasoline for spiders and crabs and, yes, octopuses.

B. It's also found in citrus.

C. For honeybees, it acts like Viagra for the banglia (bee brain).

D. Humans can eat it, too—we recommend NatraSlim Train-Wreck™.

2. Will NatraSlim TrainWreck™ help me lose weight, too?

A. Definitely.

B. There are lots of people around the world who have tried countless diets, systems, pills, videotapes, etc., in order to lose weight from their bodies.

C. But they give up from failing.

D. NatraSlim TrainWreck™ is safe, natural, and made from the South Asian fruit *Garcinia cambogia*.

E. It's basically human fruit inside of a plastic bottle.

F. A lot of people double or halve the number of push-ups they can do in an hour.

3. Where can I buy NatraSlim TrainWreck™ products?

A. NatraSlim weight loss products are not available in stores.

B. Readers of *Earn Your MBA on the Toilet* can use the promo code NUTBLOW.

C. And send a message to the pager 7764.

D. If you're not satisfied, you can throw it in the garbage because it's biodegradable (twice as compostable as 100 percent ice-cold human baby shit).

4. Will NatraSlim TrainWreck™ give me shingles?

A. It could.

BONUS ZONE!

THE FIVE BOOKS EVERY MBA SHOULD OWN

▸ *Beggar, Baker, Buyer, Bitch, Binkie, Boppo* by Connie Francis, 1972. This business psychology classic revolutionized the way we think of retail by theorizing that managers are either Binkies or Boppos. When a Boppo and a Bitch butt heads, "broductivity" busts, big-time.

▸ *The Success Syndrome* by Tyler Wenokur, 1982. Success is a disease that you want to get, so you have to try and get infected with success by never wearing a "mental condom."

▸ *Watership Down* by Richard Adams, 1972. An incredible book about a group of magical talking rabbits. Mind. Blown.

▸ *The Percival Panundrum: Making People Make People Happy* by Connor MacLanister, 1980. You'll get more done if you're positive.

▸ *The Elephant and the Dandelion: Unclocking the Business Leader Within* by Geoff Sobelle, 2012. The elephant represents your "normal"—who you are—and the dandelion is something that you're able to pick without crushing it even though you're gigantic, and that's the new you.

Here's a tip: F#ck you, I'm on my break.

CHAPTER 6

BUSINESS STATISTICS MADE EASY!

STATISTICS PLAY AN IMPORTANT ROLE in any modern business. However, statistics is definitely a weak spot in this book. It's just a very hard subject to understand. Hope this isn't a deal-breaker. Tried to get this right, but it just never really crystallized. We even had a specific guy who was going to write it or help write it, and he didn't pan out. (He didn't even really ever come back . . . it was just like, got on his bike and, "f#ck you.")

"ECONOMETRICS" It would be actually worse if we tried to teach you something that we don't understand. It would be irresponsible. It's a shitty situation. You bought the book. You deserved a real statistics chapter, no question. It's shitty all the way around because we feel that we tried our best and are at least trying to be honest now.

STATIS-TRICKS™! There are a few things that probably would still help. Sure, we f#cked up, but—"average," "mean," "median"— if you understand those, honestly? Are you going to need more than that on a realistic day-to-day basis? We hope not, because that would mean that you are *low* on the totem pole (accountant = the lowest). A CEO, trust us, is not doing that or any statistics.

So: "average" is the "overall number," how much something *usually* is, in general. "Mean" is the same. "Median," on the other hand, is one of the things we weren't able to get to. And that bugs us.

STATISTICAL FINANCIAL ANALYSIS We just feel like a jerk. It's not something we want to do, leave out this huge thing. A Japanese author would honestly probably stab himself, but that's not our culture. We hope the rest of the book makes up for it. Another thing is: if you end up failing or can't do the work, just *tell them.* Be straightforward. You got f#cked over. It wasn't your fault. You can even show them the book.

POP QUIZ!

1. **We literally don't understand this subject well enough to even come up with a single multiple choice question about it:**

    A. Again, our fault.
    B. There's other good things about this book.
    C. Are you just trying to rub it in?
    D. Go! Seriously. LOOK. AWAY.

CHAPTER 7

STRATEGY IS THE BEST STRATEGY

Don't wait to be hunted to hide.

—MOLLOY

YOUR BUSINESS STRATEGY is the means by which your company attains its goals. It is the map to success. Your "mission" is a statement that the goal of the game (not the tactics) is your "vision," headed towards the hole.

"Values" are the rules—the "what's next" of the "why"—and the "who" of the "hunh?" There can't be a Vision without a Mission, and there can't be a Mission without a real sailboat.

Are we cool, Captain?

"HOW DO I GET BETTER AT STRATEGY?"

Chess, the ultimate game of strategy, shares many parallels with business. Mastering the game can make you a better leader. Here's how to play:

SET-UP

Each player gets a large handful of pieces: pawns, castles, and many others.

Carefully line up your pieces in long rows at the back of a common checkerboard (like you might find on a porch or in the garbage).

THE OBJECT

Kill all of the other player's pieces, especially the king.

GAME PLAY

White goes first, but then black comes roaring back kicking and screaming, moving a piece of their own. Before you know it, the center of the board is just jumbled with pieces of every different stripe and variety. You'll be thinking so hard. They say that a chess Grandmaster uses more calories running a marathon than a marathon runner does! Which is easy to believe: this is war. War for pussies!

But first take a moment to think: what if those pieces had been business things? What if your opponent had been a Japanese businessman and you were hammering out a frozen

The team asks the wise old company founder, "How can we get more big clients?"

"By focusing on the clients you have," says the old man.

"We're going under," says the team.

"Seriously?!"

yogurt merger? Could you have outsmarted the old oriental gray fox? **That is what chess teaches you:** if your opponent thinks two steps ahead, think *ninety-nine hundred* steps ahead.

PRACTICE MAKES PERFECT!

Try this, throw a chess piece in the air—now say the name of the piece *and* what it does before it lands in the trash!

BETCHA DIDN'T KNOW!

A chess computer called "Deep Throat" beat Gorbachev!

Board games that will *not* build strategic-thinking skills:

- ▶ Pleasure Ball
- ▶ made-up stoner games
- ▶ Chutes and Ladders
- ▶ Operation
- ▶ My Dog Has Fleas

BONUS BUSINESS SCRATCHER!!!

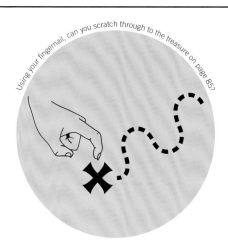

Using your fingernail, can you scratch through to the treasure on page 85?

POP QUIZ!

1. A company with no business strategy is like:

   A.   A dog with no tail

   B.   A mermaid with no tail

   C.   Two mermaids wrestling

   D.   A unicorn stabbing a centaur

2. A low-cost regional airline is an example of:

   A.   A strategy they had

   B.   That's their thing, being regional

   C.   Low-cost?

   D.   Where's this going . . . ?

3. What's your move?

(Hint: Black has a crusher.)

I feel like I'm dyin'. Gotta get this
F#CKIN' THING OFF MY HEAD!

CHAPTER 8

BUSINESS PSYCHOLOGY:
$UCCESS AND THE MINDSET OF THE
MINOTAUR-MIND™

BUSINESS PSYCHOLOGY IS ABOUT PERFORMANCE; it's about creativity; it's about motivation. And it is the key to success.

BETCHA DIDN'T KNOW!

You must think *about* your thinking and
understand your behavior to be able to do
things well in the business world.

Several years ago, researchers did a very interesting study: they put up different motivational posters in the break rooms of various businesses and measured each company's performance, and they discovered something fascinating. **Companies that displayed a poster of a harpy eagle eating a poodle quickly went bankrupt. Meanwhile, businesses that got the poster of**

41

gold medal–winning gymnast Mary Lou Retton as a faerie . . . went bananas.

Something about the emotional impact of the images affected people's ability to work! So they took the study one step further: they swapped critical features in the posters, trying to isolate which aspects were affecting people most. They created a poster of Mary Lou Retton eating a poodle and another with a harpy eagle laying a cartoon faerie-egg, and BINGO . . . both companies did about the same: great.

Performance is affected by emotion. Emotion can be provoked by sensation. This is the First Part of the Minotaur-Mind™.

Now, let's say you are giving a talk in front of a large group of executives. You're nervous. What do you do? *Picture them naked.* Over the decades, this little pearl has been validated by every known research modality.

But why? If you walked into the room to give your speech and all of the executives were *actually* naked—their *bloated bully-bags* glistening—would that calm your nerves? NO. You would lose your mind permanently.

The trick works because you gain power and status over these f#cks *in your brain!* It's all in there! You have used your own thoughts to change your reality in a manner that is empowering. Why stop there?!

Minotaur-Mind™ Part *Two*: You can use your thoughts to change your perception of any business situation into one that is more advantageous to you.

Finally, and this is the part of the system that sometimes catches people off guard: you have to drink your own pee. Sorry. Really. Everyone totally goes for the first two parts—they make a ton of sense, they seem actually helpful in a real-world sense—but you have to trust us on this last one. If you don't drink pee—a ton of pee or it won't help—the first two steps will just make things infinitely worse.

Q: What is a *life coach?* How about a personal trainer?

A: A life coach is someone who calls you every Wednesday at 9 a.m. A *personal trainer* is someone whose life coach told them to quit their last job.

There's a lot of reasons for this that are too complicated for someone without an advanced degree—you—to understand, and no amount of cartoonish diagrams will change this. (Would you want that? A diagram? A cute little cartoon man guzzling pee from a beaker with the heading "Auto-osmosis: Builds neurons for a business-happy mind!"?) You just have to trust us and start doing it right now.

Not convinced? Okay: You walk out onto a stage in front of 200 powerful execs. You picture them buck naked. *You* know (but they don't know) that you have just drank a liter of your own piss. *Now* how do you feel?

Boom. **Minotaur-Mind™ The Final Piece: You must drink your own pee.**

You should take a break. This part of the book is hard. It's a big step, and it's scary, that moment when you know that you're *absolutely* going to go through with something.

Cry, go eat a bagel, do whatever you need to do, but ask yourself: How badly do I want a Miata?

We'll see you back here soon. Let's do this.

RIP OUT THIS PAGE AND EAT IT.

Can't hack the Minotaur-Mind™? Here are some of the other popular systems for personal success that are out there in the market. Study them. Make a decision. Pick a tattoo parlor, and get started. Tonight.

POPULAR SYSTEMS FOR PERSONAL SUCCESS

THE FOUR-YEAR WORKDAY

WHAT IS IT? *The Four-Year Workday* is a personal efficiency system that was originated by a hobo named "Knuckle Dick."

WHAT IS THE SYSTEM? Doing very small amounts of work, stretched out over long periods of time.

WHAT TYPES OF JOBS WORK BEST WITH THE SYSTEM? Picking blackberries and "ballin' the jack."

IS THE SYSTEM FOR EVERYBODY? Yes, every hobo.

WHAT ARE SOME ASPECTS OF THE SYSTEM?
1. You ken do what you wat, wen you wat to.
2. Mek sure you got the canned heat!

3. No city bums.
4. I didt due one single days work in 4 years! Just pick blakberries. Yeah im ballin the jack.

YOUR DREAM$ UNLEA$HED: CRY OF THE BLACK MAMBA

HOW DOES IT WORK? Members learn a form of Gymnastics-Karate that they practice in the middle of the street, generating electrical MentalGasms™.

IS THERE A UNIFORM? Black underwear. Necktie on head.

WHO FOUNDED THE SYSTEM? Robert Michael David James.

THE BLACK MAMBA IS A TYPE OF SNAKE. DO SNAKES ACTUALLY CRY? These ones do.

ARE THERE SUCCESSFUL GRADUATES OF THE PROGRAM? Only a few: Larry Ellison, Richard Branson, and Barack O'Bannon.

BUSIN-UCCESS!

HOW DOES IT WORK? You get a packet and folders and binders in the mail.

WHAT IS THE FOCUS? You go door-to-door wearing this button that says *Busin-uccess!* and try to sell vitamins.

WHO FOUNDED THE SYSTEM? Mary Michael Doris.

WHAT IS NEEDED TO SUCCEED IN *BUSIN-UCCESS!*? A good pair of orthopedic shoes, a desire to succeed, and a refusal to look too hard at oneself.

NINE DRAGONS

WHAT IS THE BASIS OF THE SYSTEM? Only he who does not ask shall know.

CAN ANYONE JOIN? No way.

WHAT IS THE PRODUCT OR SERVICE? Nine dragons!

IS THIS GROUP INVOLVED IN ILLEGAL ACTIVITY? Maybe! No, not really. It's actually vitamins. We work with the *Busin-uccess!* girls!

PIMP DAD, WHORE DAD®

WHAT IS THE PHILOSOPHY? Economically, dads are either pimps or whores.

HOW DO YOU TELL WHICH ONE YOU ARE? One way is to ask if you are sucking dick, financially.

AND WHAT DOES A PIMP DAD DO? He's slapping people—financially—kicking them, doing blow, getting the money from weaker "whore" dads.

HAMMER TIME!
Q&A WITH DARRYL CAMARO, INVENTOR OF THE CAMARO

HOW DID YOU GET THE IDEA OF THE CAMARO?
> I wanted to make something that had never been done before.

AND HOW DID YOU DECIDE TO PUT AN EAGLE ON THE HOOD?
> That's not us, that's a Trans Am.

DOESN'T A CAMARO HAVE AN EAGLE ON THE HOOD?
> Nope. Pontiac. I just put "Camaro" on the back of my little guys.

THEY LOOK IDENTICAL. IS IT A CAMARO IN *SMOKEY AND THE BANDIT*?
> No. That's a Trans Am.

WHO PLAYED BANDIT? LEE MAJORS?
> No, umm . . . Burt . . . Burt Kwouk.

THANK YOU FOR YOUR TIME.

BONUS ZONE!

BUSINESS NAME GENERATOR

In business, your name matters *even moreso than in porno!* Just imagine if Andrew Carnegie's first name had been "Barnegie." He'd be a circus hobo's assistant!

Here's a mix-and-match chart. Give yourself a head start by choosing you a strong-sounding business name.

FIRST NAME	LAST NAME
Burt	Bushrod
Anders	Bizmarck
Bilbo	Cumdragon
Clauday	Stormhammer
Crispin	Gezelhelm
Dick	Jong II
Bartholomew	Fistwood
Captain	Icehoove
King	Enormo
Coco	Coinload
Jesus	Wang
Claude	Steelcock
Tarantula	The Kid
Sinbad	Justice
Karla	Nickelbelt

CHAPTER 9

ENTREUPEUNEURIALIASM

WHAT EXACTLY IS "ENTREPENURIEULISM"? Well, it's about opportunity: an entrepreneur is someone who takes risks to engage in a business venture, someone who crabbles together their own success.

The word "entrepreneur" comes from the French word of the same name meaning "a disabled boxer." So what are the characteristics of successful entrepreneurs? Let's go back to the beginning: the eighteenth-century French economist Pierre Menard, who coined the term, said, "The entrepreneur must possess a car, management ability, condoms, and leadership skills, and tools for making whatever the contraption is—the hot air balloon."

Entrepreneurs are **job creators**—free-thinking, roll-up-your-sleeves guys (or gals) who don't like a lot of government red tape. They prefer electric cars, bottled water, jeans, chicken pizza. Sadly, most of their money will go down the toilet or up the nose.

Entrepreneurs are often divided into several major types:

- ▶ Social: outgoing, happy, "Chatty Cathys"
- ▶ Serial: entrepreneurs who start a new company as soon as they get tired of the old blown-out one
- ▶ Chinchilla type: sleep during the day and work at night
- ▶ Lifestyle entrepreneurs: The term "lifestyle" generally refers to swinging—attending group sex parties where food is served. In this case, though, it refers to a type of entrepreneur.

Q: What's the difference between a copyright and a trademark? What about a patent?

A: *Now you're talkin'!* Hey everybody, check out little Mister Businessman here!

Because **entreupenialism** implies a "creative destruction" of existing business norms, it's best taught by example. Here are case studies of successful businesses started by entrepreneurs.

CORBEPT

When Richard Dale James got out of prison, he knew he wanted to be a doctor, but he knew also that the only way to work with bone marrow was to get your hands dirty. So he founded Corbept. His uncle and grandpa provided the start-up money, but the first years were lean: "We'd be at the office for twelve or fourteen hours a day, just staring at each other, jacking off, taking naps. I built a motorcycle from a kit. Then the phone rang—we were going public . . . or we had got bought out, one of the big ones. Super exciting."

SJOLIANDRIENDRIE

Brida Chebaux knew that being a model wasn't enough. She also had to make panties that fit a woman's natural lines while letting the front breathe. That's why she started Sjoliandriendrie (the "sj" is pronounced like a "hswa" sound). Using money from her uncle and grandpa, she manufactured the first hundred panties in her basement. Two years later, she got a call from Jean-Marc Pegutier from PiPi Couture—they wanted everyone to be wearing the special vented panties. She was a billionaire.

CHICKENHAWK DEFENSE BALL CORP

"We had a kill-ball with a twenty mile radius," says Trevor Dan Mark, Jr. "We knew we had a killing machine, we just didn't know what to kill—a dog? What?" That's when the phone rang; it was a government asking for hundreds of the death balls. "We looked at each other and our faces were frozen in a red crying mask—of happiness."

POLE SNAKE

"With the pole snake, your toilet is gonna give up." With those words, a late-night legend was born. Hannah Klein and her sister Shoshona took their experience of being raised on a commune to add a muscular twist to an old idea, the plunger. The Pole Snake could root a Class V shitball in three flat—blow it fifty feet out a smokestack. The competition was dead, *if* Pole Snake could line up funding—which they did. The Internet. Now they're millionaires.

Business legend John D. Rockefeller, if he were here today

CHINADERMITAXI

Before Ron Zhen Hao came up with the idea, no one in China had ever stuffed a real panda bear and sold it to children. Now every panda in China has been stuffed. The results? Big-time respect for Hao's family: huge banquets and weddings. Just round-the-clock deep Chinese cultural celebrations. Really interesting stuff, but *intense*. And they eat *everything* there. Frogs, you name it . . .

PROFILES OF SMALL BUSINESS:
GABRIEL JOHN WEISERT, FOUNDER, DRESS FOR SUKKE$$

HOW'S THE COMPANY?
> Today is not a good day because I hit a kid with my Jet Ski. Hopefully it could still be that it was a dolphin that I hit, but the tests aren't back yet.

HOW DID YOU GET STARTED?
> I was always into clothes, but that's hard to think about right now.

DID YOU ALWAYS WANT TO BE A SMALL BUSINESS OWNER?
> I don't know, but I know I always never wanted to hit a living person with my Jet Ski. I always knew that.

WHAT ARE THE HARD THINGS ABOUT SMALL BUSINESSES?
> Sometimes you're just having fun and—wham!—you hear a bump, and your life changes.

WHAT'S NEXT FOR DRESS FOR SUKKE$$?
> It could be really bad. I might be going to prison. They had me super drunk at the scene.

ANY FINAL WORDS?
> A Jet Ski is not a toy. It's a dangerous killing machine.

POP QUIZ!

1. **Who would make the best entrepreneur?**

   A. The Bionic Woman
   B. The Hulk
   C. The Thing
   D. Swamp Thing

2. **All successful entrepreneurs share this one feature:**

   A. Opposable thumbs
   B. Bifid penis
   C. "Pear" body shape
   D. Prehensile tail

3. **A "social" entrepreneur:**

   A. Uses relationships to invent inventions
   B. Has a "business" voice and a high-pitched "chipmunk" voice
   C. Is about enough to give you a big ole seizure
   D. Lives in organized underground clans

4. **Which is the correct spelling of "entrepreneur"?**

   A. Entreprenuer
   B. Entrepenuer
   C. Entrepreneur
   D. Entrepeneur

CHAPTER 10

LEADERSHIP:
HARNESSING YOUR INNER DARTH GANDHI

The key to leadership is to take the mo . . .

—FRAGMENT FROM THE TWELFTH-
CENTURY *EPIC OF SHURSAHESH*

THE WORD "LEADER" DERIVES FROM the Greek word δουζηεβας, which translates to "jhvkjablkjrf"—a baffling riddle from the past. They believed that the first leader was a wolf animal that came into town and suckled a human woman's breast, and *that's how Rome was founded!*

Scientists now know that there have been leaders all the way back to the cavemen, who were known to have delegated basic tasks like stacking giant huge piles of blown-out tree parts.

A leader needs condoms.

We all know leadership when we see it, but what is it, really? Welp, scientists now know that a leader is a *person* who:

- . . . makes decisions.
- . . . motivates others to believe in a cause or idea.
- . . . is not in the hospital.
- . . . breaks pencils, figurines, or glassware.
- . . . "smells" possibilities.
- . . . doesn't flame newbs on Internet forums.
- . . . knows their own "flip-out point."
- . . . doesn't look at their own butt h#le with a mirror or iPhone.
- . . . is not super-sarcastic.
- . . . never drinks to excess to excess.
- . . . has a rich baritone voice.
- . . . has a bifid penis.
- . . . doesn't take notes.
- . . . doesn't usually have *huge* tits.
- . . . has no problem changing underwear.
- . . . doesn't make their own yogurt or do beekeeping.

- ▶ . . . has "emotional intelligence."
- ▶ . . . doesn't get seasick.
- ▶ . . . has been in a war or wants to be in a war.
- ▶ . . . doesn't ride a recumbent bicycle or unicycle.
- ▶ . . . has more than four teeth but not buckteeth.
- ▶ . . . was/is an astronaut.
- ▶ . . . speaks clearly, not mashing words together.
- ▶ . . . might take medicine but not be in a hospital.
- ▶ . . . doesn't think certain foods make him "sleepy."
- ▶ . . . doesn't giggle or tickle or be ticklish.
- ▶ . . . gets diarrhea, but doesn't have to know it.
- ▶ . . . knows computers.
- ▶ . . . can memorize any state capital.
- ▶ . . . is willing to die for a cause, but is not in the hospital.
- ▶ . . . doesn't mouth the words while others talk to them.
- ▶ . . . has a thin wallet, not overstuffed.
- ▶ . . . is not allergic to bees.
- ▶ . . . can have a cane, or be in a sling, but not more than that.
- ▶ . . . doesn't collect stickers or bottle caps.
- ▶ . . . is a great teacher but not stuck in a dead-end teaching job.
- ▶ . . . doesn't eat food off other people's plates.
- ▶ . . . doesn't have a lot of BAND-AIDS® on their face.
- ▶ . . . brings different races of people together to white-water raft.
- ▶ . . . doesn't always bail on Thanksgiving.
- ▶ . . . cuts a ribbon with giant scissors.
- ▶ . . . can ride horses.
- ▶ . . . is not afraid of mice or spiders.
- ▶ . . . does not "shriek."
- ▶ . . . has a coconut ass.

Not only does every leader possess every trait above, but . . .

No person in history who is missing any of the above traits has ever led anything, even down to the dumbest little model-railroading club.

 CUT THE LIST OUT AND IRON IT ON TO YOUR BANDANA. DO IT.

Q: Can you be a leader of "nothing" and no one know it?

A: *It depends.*

Congratulations! DECLARE A STATE OF PLAGUE AND CLOSE THE TOWN! You've just finished the Principles of Leadership! But how do you know if *you've* "got the stuff" to be a leader? Why not take a test and find out? The business world has embraced a number of tools that can help you know what you're made of. Check it out:

SELF-ASSESSMENT

Personal self-assessment focuses on *personality* and can be done informally by asking yourself three probing questions when confronted with any work situation:

1.   "Would I like me if I saw me doing that?"

2.   "Would me like you if he saw I doing me?"

3.   "How does me do a better job?"

It is that last question, of course, that is most important: "How *does* me do a better job?"

Studies show that we naturally resist even positive change, but executives who regularly self-assess and adjust their behavior tend to be more satisfied in their work. Change can be both personal or professional and can range from taking a "birdbath" before meetings to wearing a different bomber jacket, spray-painting the Miata, even getting a Cockalofin™ for Linda and the stepkids: change.

I tried every morning to write down a list of twenty things
that I didn't like about myself, but the list was always,
"I hate my butt, I hate my butt, I hate my butt . . . "
—Henry Ford

There are also several standardized self-assessment tests that can target specific areas of need:

- Why Am I Such an Assh#le? (WAISAA)
- Wow You're SO Great at Everything (WYSGAE Sarcasm Self-Test)
- Everything I Do Turns to Shit (Minnesota OIDAGIB Wet Blanket/Downer Index)

These are often available online or from your HR department and can provide the self-data you need to make a quick lateral move from mailroom to mailroom.

To get you started, here is the standard in the industry, the **Personal Business Leadership Inventory Test Assessment Scale Exam (PBLITASE).** Take the test on the following page and tally up your score.

ZEN-O-NOMICS

A man takes a bong hit and gets an idea to start a chain of frozen yogurt parlors. The next morning, he RIDES his bike to work.

PERSONAL LEADERSHIP ASSESSMENT

1. **My greatest fear as a business leader is:**
   A. Fear itself
   B. Stuck in my shirt (can't unbutton shirt)
   C. Kicking so much ass I go to the Olympics Jail
   D. Orangutan crashes my Ferrari into a tollbooth

2. **The biggest element of my past/upbringing that may be holding me back as a leader is:**
   A. My uncles died during my sentencing
   B. My lack of emotions, intelligence, and emotional intelligence
   C. Partying too much for words
   D. College professor who wrote "God #3" on my back in lipstick

3. **The image that best represents how I think of myself as a leader is:**
   A. Ship captain with a telescope
   B. A jockey on a monkey with a saddle
   C. A river otter with tons of friends
   D. Human cannonball being blasted through a dog-shit waterfall

4. **When I'm in a stressful situation as a leader, I tend to:**
   A. Take a deep breath and try to hold it forever
   B. Trace a decision tree in the air
   C. Silently mouth the word "omo"
   D. Close my eyes and mentally put on my Darth Vader shit

5. **My greatest source of personal strength as a leader is:**
   A. Vita-min F
   B. My wives, children, and boyfriend
   C. Shark-tooth necklace
   D. Hummus

Tally it up! Counting vowels and face cards as two, add up your letters using numerical proxies. If you scored less than five, PUSH THIS BOOK BETWEEN YOUR LEGS AND INTO THE "BOWL" OF THE TOILET (if unable to flush the book down, cover it with a mound of toilet paper and go camping in your backyard for a couple of days). Otherwise, come on down to the executive lounge, you just may be CorOffMat (corner-office material)!

BUSINESS PROFILES IN COURAGE: BILBO BAGGINS

POSITION: CEO, Bilbollionaires Corp.

AGE: 500

BY THE NUMBERS:
Increased revenue by an estimated $50M in gold pieces during first year as CEO.

INTERESTING FACT:
Allergic to criticism.

BIGGEST OBSTACLE TO SUCCESS:
Trolls, elves, giant spiders, a man who can change shape into a bear, goblins, eagles, Gollum.

ADVICE TO NEW CEOS:
"The team is key to supporting a product that will succeed. People—dwarves and hobbits and wizards—are the most important resource of your business."

BIG BREAK:
Hired by Gandalf to jump-start a treasure-recovery widget to address huge negative ROI in terms of elves being mowed down.

TEACHABLE MOMENT:
"After we acquired Smaug's treasure, I could've done a better job of bringing opposing sides to the table by using a stolen heirloom jewel as leverage. It hurt; especially my friendship with Thorin, who got stabbed."

BIGGEST GROWTH AREA FOR LEADERS:
Successful marketing-focused leaders understand more than strategy and products; they understand the power of invisibility.

PROUDEST (NONBUSINESS) MOMENT:
Quitting smoking using the patch.

BONUS ZONE!

GREAT SPEECHES IN BUSINESS HISTORY

Blaine Cardoza is considered the father of inspirational leadership communication. Here is his keynote speech to Little Black Sambo's Restaurant Chain, Inc., Eau Claire, Wisconsin, June 7, 1964:

HELLO SAMBO'S . . . I SAID . . . HEELLLLOOOO SAAMM-MMBOOO'S . . . Yeah, all right! That's more like it! Whew! Yeah! Are you feeling good, Sambo's?! Huh?! Are you?! I said: Are. You. Feeling. GOOOOODDD SAMBOOOOO'S INCORPORATED! Whew! All right! It is great to be here with you, Sambo's. Is it great to be me with you?! Thank you! Okay.

Reggie, you want to put up our first slide? What's that curve right there? That, my friends, is Sambo's earning for Q1 and 2, 1964—can you say "new record"? There's no stopping you now. Nothing can stop Sambo's now! There is no one thing that could ever stop this restaurant, except for a black swan . . . But that wouldn't stop Sambo's. The food is too good, the sundaes are too good to be TRUUUEEE! Hang on, I'm getting a message here . . . there is looting in the downtown. Everyone calm down. There is looting in the downtown . . . near here, near the hotel. Let me . . . let's get to the point, and just get to the meat here so you guys can get to your party!!! You gotta blow your horn, Sambo's. You. Gotta. Blow. Your horn. Sambo's has gotta blow its horn and know who it is, what it's about as a company—its core principles. You're SAMBO'S! Don't forget that. I'm not Sambo's, YOU ARE! Don't forget that 'cause it's in every pancake that you churn out and every glob of delicious . . . I'm hearing . . . that's gunfire, Sambo's. There's gunfire in Eau Claire. Hell has come to Eau Claire, Sambo's. Hell tonight in the streets. Wear your guns. Wear your aprons. They're gonna be comin' out of the sewers tonight, Sambo's. Thank you.

Leadership, A Poem

BY CEO GEOFF T.

When an Indian brave
Rallies his men
That's-a-leadership!
When a president gives
An amazing radio speech
That's-a-leadership!
When an astronaut (Wally Schirra)
Stops to talk to a child
That's-a-leadership!
When a country gives her people
Hope, not handouts
That's-a-leadership!
L-L-L-LEADERSHIP

CHAPTER 11

BUSINESS ETHICS:
LOL

WHAT IS *BUSINESS ETHICS*? HA HA HA good question! But the bigger question is WHO GIVES A SHIT?!

Seriously, major changes have been made since the economic meltdown of 2008. ALL CORPORATIONS NOW STRONGLY EMBRACE A SET OF GUIDING MORAL PRINCIPLES. To the hilt.

Proof is on the next page.

Hola! I'm Learning Donny from *Chicken Coops for Dumbshits*. Fillin' in for Dave!

GOLDMAN SACHS' CODE OF CONDUCT
PRE-2008

OUR VI$ION

KICK ASS! F#CK YAY.

OUR VALUES

- **People** *Yeah. F#CK PEOPLE: $$$*
- **Cu$tomer Focu$** *Show me the money baby! F#CK! I'm HARD. $$$*
- **Performance** *You got it right, motherf#cker! I CAN MULTIORGASM WHENEVER I WANT $$$$ KICK ASS!*
- **Integrity** *I CAN'T HEEEEAAAARRRR YOU! YEAH. F#CK YEAH!*
- **Re$pect** *Value all f#ckin' . . . WOO-HOO! Trillions and trillions. Lamborghini.*
- **Entrepreneur$hip** *Seize all opportunitie$ to f#ckin' HA HA HA. $$$*

The core value$ and principle$ $et forth in our Code are a reflection OF THE FACT THAT WE ARE MINOTAUR$ AND CANNOT BE KILLED! F#ck you.

GOLDMAN SACHS' CODE OF CONDUCT
2012

<u>OUR VISION</u>

Help baby pandas find their mommies.

<u>OUR VALUES</u>

- ▶ **People** *Treat all human beings as if they were living things.*
- ▶ **Customer Focus** *We will literally lick your bottom from how sorry we are.*
- ▶ **Performance** *We will measure our success in Happy Bux™.*
- ▶ **Integrity** *If we feel like gambling with the retirement savings of an entire generation, we will call the help line, do deep breathing, or take a walk.*
- ▶ **Respect** *Just basically more of the above. Helping.*
- ▶ **Entrepreneurship** *Invent puppy insulin.*

The core values and principles set forth in our Code are a reflection of the fact that we are not minotaurs. We are not immortal. We're just people. People helping people help pandas. There. We're f#ckin' eunuchs now. Ya happy?

GREAT! READY FOR SOME ETHICS CASE STUDIES?

Ethical case studies are an important way to practice the principles you've learned. Remember that ethics is not like math—every answer is right. Fire away!

CASE STUDY #1

As the senior vice president of a major corporation, you have been charged with overseeing product development for an underwater dynamite-ball that blows up coral reefs and sprays a poison rainbow.

Profits are down by 1,000,000,000 percent year to year, and your boss is breathing down your neck, whenever the two of you make love in the LaGuardia Airport Hotel, formerly The Wyndham Garden Hotel®. Your boss was formerly a Navy SEAL, and formerly a model for Timberland® boots.

Some staff have complained privately to you that your boss, whom we'll call "Black Donna," has been making racist comments to them. Donna has confided to you that she is Asian, but she's asked you not to keep this a secret. You were under the assumption that s/he was Native American.

Ready? Go:

_____

_____

_____

CASE STUDY #2

You are the VP of Marketing for Muchos Widgetz, and last Thursday you think you saw your boss, Mark, set fire to a cop car (it was either a regular-sized cop car and he was a giant, or he was normal human-sized and the car was tiny). At 4:05 p.m. he took a train to a fundraiser for Race Rapids, a charity that sends white people on white-water rafting trips with mixed-race widows of Hurricane Daniel.

When you returned home you took mushrooms and then finished two Sudokus and had three Huge Orgasms before falling asleep at 1:02 a.m. with your pants shredded into shorts-pants.

What time will your mental train crash into Mark's real train?

_____

_____

_____

CASE STUDY #3

You are the head of human resources at a factory that makes duck shirts. You've recently fired an employee (whom we'll call "Deaf Larry") because he missed several shifts without calling in.

Larry is also the defendant in an (unrelated) sexual harassment lawsuit filed by the zoo.

Now Deaf Larry has applied for a position at a different company—your biggest competitor, Señor Quack-N-Pussy—and he's listed you as a reference.

While you are using the bathroom, Larry text-messages you to say he's terminally ill, but then his co-workers come to you (while you're still in the bathroom) to say that Larry may be lying about everything and have a fake passport.

Remember: you have already terminated Larry. The decision before you now is whether or not to *terminate* Larry.

Y / N (circle one)

CHAPTER 12

IF JOHN WAYNE AND YODA HAD A BABY:
ATTRIBUTES OF THE GREAT MANAGER

WHAT MAKES A GREAT MANAGER? Is it the same as what makes a great leader?

NO! F#CK NO!! ARE YOU CRAZY!!! God.

You know what? This learning session is over. Why? 'Cause you're acting like a complete f#ckin' jerk, that's why.

Seriously. See you the next time you have to take a shit.

WELCOME BACK!

Trust me, that little Yoda moment back there will help you. You needed it. You're back, and you're hungry. *That* was effective management.

SEE WHAT WE DID?

We motivated you, brought the best out of you, and challenged you, and we couldn't have done it if we hadn't been *mindful*—if we hadn't learned what makes *you* unique, what makes *you* tick. Not John or Sally or Pablo—you. You're a dick. You are. You're an old-school, punch-in-the-fish-tank dick. Some people aren't dicks, and we would have dealt with them a whole different way (either with "'Boo-hoo I can't do it' . . . GROW UP!" or "Not bad! Wow, what's next from you!"). *That* is effective management.

NOW TRY THIS

A great way to think about "the perfect manager" is to imagine if John Wayne and Yoda had a baby. Put aside whether that's actually possible or whether getting Yoda pregnant would be a form of "playing God," and just imagine the skills that the baby would possess. Keep bringing your mind back to the baby, itself, not the conception part. Lots of people find themselves mentally stuck on the image of John Wayne and Yoda mating. That is not the take-away here.

The baby would be wise, tough, empathetic, and powerful.

It's tempting to imagine Yoda wearing a cowboy get-up and John Wayne rushing in and sweeping him off of his feet and kissing him, Yoda, on the mouth and neck. You're just wasting your time thinking about that. Could they have a baby? We don't know. Of course they could. John Wayne had a penis; Yoda had something for sure that was pretty futuristic. Get over it. You wanna pull up his dress and look? You're missing the point.

This is just a thought exercise to highlight the leadership traits that the baby might have. If it were viable. If it weren't a monster. Mental images of Yoda in labor (probably on his planet, Dagobah) and actually giving birth to the sickly green swamp cowboy are just so far from the point we're trying to make.

Who delivers the baby? Luke? One of Wayne's cowpoke drinking buddies?

Doesn't matter.

What matters? A person—a man, a woman, a child—who had John Wayne's gritty take-charge attitude and Yoda's calm, Zen-like strength and searing insight: that guy would be a great manager. Maybe the greatest ever.

WHAT OTHER THINGS ARE THERE?

The effective manager must be ready for anything. But here are the crucial skills of the guys and gals at the top:

PLANNING/PARTY PLANNING This means having a plan *before* something happens. If that thing is a party, then it is considered "party planning." Other things you could plan might include a meeting, a merger . . . those would be two of the big ones.

ORGANIZING Do we really have to do this? It's just like it sounds. It's f#cking organizing.

KICKING ASS This is the intangible. The black card. Lady luck. The death's head. The dead man's hand. Batman. When you fight someone, and you "kick their ass," you never actually *hit their butt* with your foot. Kicking ass is a feeling you get—whether in the boardroom or the basement of your mom's house.

DON'T TAKING NO FOR AN ANSWER This is something you can practice very effectively with a parrot, a bag of peanut butter pretzels, and a Wiffle-ball bat.

SHOTOKAN/KENPO/TIGER STYLE KARATE These are the disciplines that make your hands like a cactus and your mind like a cactus. Kenpo has some of the best tattoos (panther scratching you, Chinese characters, etc.).

LEADING BY EXAMPLE Especially if you are absolutely horrible with words, MIME IT OUT!

DECISIONAL WAFFLING Here's a little secret (a filthy, disgusting little tramp of a secret): you often get more done by failing to decide, by *waffling*. Hang back. Confident decision making is the hobgoblin of baby-headed people.

Are you still thinking about the Duke making love to Yoda?! Shame on you.

ARE WE THROUGH YET?

Almost! It's time for the dreaded **Management Perspectives Project!** Don't worry, it'll be fun. Pick one of the following and get started!

1. Build a lawnmower with someone from another "culture."
2. Make a map of your whole house.
3. Paint a mental figurine.
5. Website would probably be too hard.
4. Coordinate a peace-pipe ceremony between the ostrich people and the llama people.
3. No one's done 4-D chess.
2. Open study.

ALMOST THERE!

Congratulations! By completing the project, you have passed through the primary rite of passage required of all first-year MBA candidates. Now simply mail the results to Dr. de Selby, Business Institutes at Dong Ha. Then go to any ATM, and speaking clearly into the security mirror, say, "Tell me what I deserve." Your final grade should pop up on the screen!

GREAT MANAGERS IN TV/MOVIE HISTORY

YODA (*Star Wars 2*) Top dog in the management cinesphere. A weird "creature" with a solid blend of tough love, philosophical "mind puzzles," and Old West grittiness, played just right by Linda Hunt.

MR. MIYAGI (*Karate Kid*) East meets West excellence. Gives a car to his student as a bonus, but otherwise a strict follower of "Do it right the first time!"

THE BIONIC MAN (*The Bionic Man*) The ultimate "hands-on" manager took pumping iron to a new level when he beat the shit out of Bigfoot.

ZEN-O-NOMICS

A flight attendant tells a man in business class that he's not allowed to smoke; he tells her that he could buy the whole airline and fire her.

"You'll have to catch me first," she says and parachutes out of the plane.

STRINGFELLOW HAWKE (*Airwolf*) The pilot of Airwolf, the most advanced military helicopter this side of Blue Thunder. Would be great as the manager of a large helicopter. Great pilot. Great guy.

GANDHI (*Gandhi*) The main character in the movie *Gandhi* is a man named "Gandhi" who is the classic "98-pound weakling." He starts pumping iron and getting focused, mentally, then garners a huge ragtag band of followers. The shoot-out in the end is priceless. Management style: Lawful Good.

CAVEMAN #2 (*Quest for Fire*) A quirky band of cavemen starts out obsessed with sex, but then one of them (they don't have names) starts to get serious about how they should be focusing on getting fire, not just f#cking, pig style. The first great managers?? :)

B. J. (*B. J. and the Bear*) This take-no-for-an-answer truck driver multitasks a successful long-haul business while gently caring for a mischievous Chimpanese.

SIX SIGMA: A NEW MANAGEMENT DISCIPLINE

In 1972, Glenn and Dick Spicer (no relation), engineers at Billy Plastic Walkie-Talkie Labs in Princeton, New Jersey, created a system for reducing manufacturing errors by creating uniform standards for quality control, but they added a crucial twist: employees who mastered the system would be awarded colored karate belts.

They called their system Five Vagina (because "vagina" is the eighth letter in the Greek alphabet). Walkie-talkies that achieved a Five Vagina rating would crumble to pieces 0.123456 percent of the time. In 1982, Dick perished and the system was generalized and the name updated to Six Sigma. The core principles are as follows:

1. Try as hard as you can to make as good of a walkie-talkie as you can.

2. "Good enough" is not good enough.

3. When it comes to walkie-talkies, it's not enough to be second best.

4. When public speaking, try and picture the audience naked.

5. God don't make junk.

Employees who mastered all six of the above were awarded a green belt. Anyone who gave 110 percent was bumped up to a black belt. This system was put into place for major corporations such as DishWipe and f#ckWad.

 BETCHA DIDN'T KNOW!

Six Sigma graduates with a black belt should not try to fight black belts of other disciplines. They could be killed.

Q: I'm a green belt in Five Vagina, what belt am I in Six Sigma?
A: Blue-green. (Source: "What color is my Five Vagina belt now?" Dave Shad, Jr., *Bus. Sci. Fuc. Sht.*, June, 1983)

POP QUIZ!

1. **A good manager _____ his employees:**

    A. Captures
    B. Cherishes
    C. Sprays
    D. Kills

2. **If you score a zero on the Management Perspectives Project:**

    A. You can't think.
    B. You can only think "duh."
    C. You are more of a *checkers person* than a *chess person*.
    D. You've got major major problems.

3. **Napoleon said that great managers:**

    A. Are born, not made
    B. Have some traits right out of the vagina, but can develop others
    C. Can be "made" years after leaving the vagina
    D. Have a vagina and a penis

4. **According to management guru Antoine Crespi, if dolphins had hands, they would be:**

    A. Second
    B. Fifth
    C. Fourth
    D. Number one

5. **Match the action with the management style:**

    A. A boss who asks her secretary to inject testosterone into her thigh
    B. A chef who stomps his feet and screams at his staff, "I wish I'd never been born!"
    C. A prison guard who apologizes for using the "n-word" by giving his deputies Baskin Robbins Big Cake! cards

    i.   Delegative Management
    ii. Autocratic Management
    iii. Democratic Management

CHAPTER 13

FAKE IT TILL YOU MAKE IT:
HOW TO ACT AND DRESS LIKE YOU'RE SOMEBODY

Avoid excessive blinking and wild eye movements.

—JOHN SELMER DIX, *WITH WINGS AS EAGLES*

IN THE BUSINESS WORLD, you are your hugest asset. How you carry yourself can be the difference between "I'm rich!" and "I'm a hunchback's *assistant's* life coach." Let's get you started on the path toward looking and acting like the person you want to be.

HYGIENE AND GROOMING

In business, it's not "if you take a shower," it's "*when* you take a shower." Victor Faygo, Chief User Experience Evangelist of Beanie Boyby,™ actually had a shower in his Subaru Brat!

When showering, concentrate on cleaning your own body and hair. It's not necessary to bring other objects into the shower to clean them, too.

Fingernails should be kept clean and short unless you have a *legitimate shot* at getting into the *Guinness Book of World Records* (be honest with yourself).

Hair should be worn above the belt or braided into a vest. Men, your eyes should be visible. Don't "hide" things in your hair (radio, wallet).

For brushing teeth, a toothbrush is best, but a hairbrush will do. Toothpaste is yummy, but not for eating!

QUICKTIP™ A little WD-40 can really make the eyebrows pop!

CAN PEOPLE SMELL ME?

Yes they can, but at a microscopic level. This is the science of pheromones: the secret smell signal of succe$$. What message do these secret chemicals send? The message that you are ready to be mated with by a bigger creature, a *cave person*. But are these ancient signals still being sent today? Yes they are, and you need to know about them. For example, if you start getting an erection in a meeting where nothing—not one thing—is sexy, you're smelling someone's chemical. They're dominant now, and instead of thinking about the meeting, you're being controlled.

 BETCHA DIDN'T KNOW

Women can get erections, too, even
though they are tee-niny! :)

WHAT CAN I DO ABOUT IT?

Be aware. If you're mindful that subtle, chemical status-transactions are occurring at all times, and you suspect someone, you can then say to the person, "I know what you're doing and stop it." If they don't tone down the "f#ck me" odor, put cotton balls in each nose, look them in the eye, and say, "I mean it, I mean business."

WHAT ABOUT PEOPLE JUST PLAIN SMELLING YOU, NOT IN A MICROSCOPIC WAY?

No one said getting an MBA would be easy! It is possible, they now know, to just be smelly without it being a secret chemical signal. General rule? *If you can smell yourself, it may be time to get a convertible!*

DRESS FOR SU$$ESS

In the world of business, how you look *matters*—deals are made and deals are broken on first impressions. Your clothes need to be sharp but generally conservative; **business dress** is usually divided into three major types.

1. BUSINESS ATTIRE

This is how you will usually be dressed at work: for men, this means slacks, collared shirt, and work shoes; for women, a blouse with a skirt or pants and "nice" shoes. There's a lot of leeway here, so follow these helpful guidelines.

Never wear a thong *outside* of your pants (ladies, this goes for you too!).

Gentlemen: a sport coat should have two or three buttons; never button the bottom one unless there is tenting of the penis-pole.

How to tie a clip-on tie

A colored handkerchief in the breast or back pocket can add a nice accent. (Careful: purple means "idiot.")

Women: skirts should go down past your fingertips when your arms are at your sides. If you have *extremely* short arms, remember that your nu-nu should not be visible.

Never iron your skin directly.

Gloves should never be worn alone (only with pants, shirt, and shoes).

Always wear *two* shoes.

Costumes should only be worn on special occasions!

2. FORMAL BUSINESS ATTIRE

For men, this still means a chasuble of marten skin tied with an elf-hair cincture. Below the waist, barbarian trousers or cross-gartered hose—with the stomach hair in a gold dangle or penumbrian braid.

For women, be prepared to wear a long-lace tunic dress with fur trumpet sleeves, laced at the bodice to allow you to really get air.

Formal dress is rare, thank god! Reserved for the most important meetings and presentations. On Fridays, you may be lucky enough to wear . . .

3. BUSINESS CASUAL

Think *Quest for Fire.* Employees can be naked or can cover their bodies in trash, food, mud.

Morning Mirror Check!: Are my pants inside-out?

OPTIMAL HEALTH FOR THE BUSINESS LIFESTYLE

EXERCISE

There's a famous story about John Jacob Toyota, inventor of the Honda Civic. A reporter asked him if he had to give up either his StairMaster or pumping iron, which one he would choose. "Are you crazy?" he answered. "I'd probably go nuts. Probably try to f#ck a minotaur. Ha ha ha." That's how important physical fitness is to the top guys: it's not *everything*, it's the whole . . . it *is* everything!

MIX UP YOUR WORKOUTS WITH A
BLEND OF THESE BASICS

AEROBICS This does not mean dancing in front of the TV, it means reaching your "target heart rate" for greater than 20 minutes. Many of your favorite activities are aerobic: running, swimming, cycling. But others are not: LazerTag™, kite snurfing, hump gliding.

Q: Is hot-dogging aerobic?
A: It depends.

MUSCLE BUILDING Big muscles increase your strength, help you look great, and boost metabolism. Get buff by weight lifting ("pumping iron"), doing isotonic exercises (such as taking a pretend shit), or engaging in vigorous work (like digging an animal grave).

ZEN-O-NOMICS

A man calls customer service for a major shoe company but is kept on hold until he finally hangs up. He later realizes that the "phone" was actually a huge black candle.

KARATE The Dalai Lama once said that Chuck Norris should get two Nobel Prizes: one for economics, one for literature, and one for kicking ass. The same goes for the business world. Shotokan, Tiger Style, or Kenpo. Pick one.

OH, AND . . . A few pushups before a meeting can add confidence and tone. If you can make your muscles bulge so much that your clothing rips apart, do it. But there's no halfway here . . .

DIET

A business career can be very stressful. Optimum performance means eating right. Start with the **food pyramid:**

GRAINS/MEAT/CHICKENS/BANANAS One item for every box of the pyramid multiplied by the time you spend on yourself every day. If you do the math right, you might be surprised to learn that you should be eating many chickens every day . . . *and about 20 bananas!*

For the busy exec, **eating smaller amounts more frequently** can give all-day energy without the crash, especially with low-glycemic-index foods like Cashew-BloNutz™. Here's a model menu for the healthy executive:

- ▶ **Meal #1, 7 a.m.** Hummus (Arabian peanut butter) and apple slices; CashewBloNutz™; two bananas.
- ▶ **Meal #2, 10 a.m.** Chicken parts; one banana leading to another two bananas; fruit roll-up.
- ▶ **Meal #3, Noon.** Pancakes; barbecued goat; chickens; bananas; more CashewBloBaz™.
- ▶ **Meal #4, 2 p.m.** Couldn't eat.

- **Meal #5, 4 p.m.** Back on the horse. Ate a horse, a backpack, a chicken, a banana, and two Tuboli's of CashewNana™.
- **Meal #6, 4:26 p.m.** Fifty bananas. Can't swallow my ChikenGazm™.
- **Meal #9, ?:??** Lick out five-layer dip. Can't piss.
- **Eagle #X, 1:68 a.m.** Not forming new memories. Try to enter a stranger's home. Shot in leg.

BETCHA DIDN'T KNOW!

A bowl of Halloween candy has about the same amount of calories as brainstorming!

HOW TO ACT

Social life in the top echelons of the business world can be a minefield if you don't know how the 1 percent behave.

> **QUIKTIP!™** "Wow, you have a huge tongue" can be a nice disarming opener.

First, you must be aware of status: you are constantly sending and receiving subtle signals that establish your position in the social hierarchy. Climb the ladder with these tips:

- Find the alpha male: Go to him, arch your back, and say (or sign), "I'm submissive to you FOR NOW."
- Never slouch; instead walk with an accordion-like bounce, with the knuckles hanging low and facing forward. Turn the torso and head as one unit.

- Never. Ever. Blink your eyes.
- While shaking a superior's hand, do a deep knee-bend. An inferior's: a tasteful pelvic thrust.
- And again—if you can do it—flex your muscles hard enough to rip your pants and shirt to shreds.

One pharmaceutical exec says he kept his confidence up by secretly wearing a police badge under his coat that said "SHERIFF OF DIABETES."

> **QUIKTIP!™** If you are a passenger in your boss's car, and it is a convertible, be prepared, when she puts the top down, to feel like the roof is ripping right off. Scream with your mouth shut if you have to, because the first time you sit in a fancy rich car like that and the roof starts peeling up, you will literally hear screaming and not know that it's you, and if you do that—if you scream like that—you WILL be fired.

Social interactions and meetings will be part of your daily life. Try these:

- When someone tells you their name, repeat it to them three times, point to your head, and say, "got it."
- Men, curtseying is not just for women anymore. Try it!
- If you are having personal problems, lead with them.
- Only play the cancer card if more than thirty minutes late for something.
- And for the truly confident: try flicking your business card into the client's drink and saying, "My whole family was born to win."

My most awkward moment? We were meeting a very important client, and I put out my hand to shake. He had a hook for a hand! The hook went through my palm, and he was swinging me around and around. Luckily he had a sense of humor about it.

—Richard S., Junior Exec.

A word about blimp etiquette: Most MBAs will still get to travel by blimp. A blimp or "inflatable traveling gas log" has the same rules as a hot air balloon: no cheroots, crampons, or sparklers. No dogs or hard drugs. And the toilets can be funny, so t.p. only please! Never put a tampon in a blimp toilet (see "The Hindenberg").

A Real Situation™

Q: Brett has a ferret in her cubicle, and a knife. The musk is overpowering. Thoughts?

A: HR should bring a bang stick and a hoop bag. The ball's in Brett's court now.

Congratulations, you just ruined a whole book.

(see page 39)

POP QUIZ!

1. **When unsure of the attire at a business function:**
   A. It's your fault.
   B. Wear nothing but Rollerblades™.
   C. Stay in the Miata.
   D. Take a hostage.

2. **Pumping iron makes you _____ than Liquid Chicken™.**
   A. More buff
   B. Less buff
   C. Buff is buff, no matter what
   D. Cry more

3. **After a report of sexual harassment has been made by an employee, a manager should:**
   A. Give a "thumbs-up"
   B. Physically examine the employee
   C. Feign deafness
   D. Tip the cap and say, "touché"

4. **The following are examples of "high status" behaviors:**
   A. Throwing poo
   B. Standing on someone else's tie
   C. Smoking more than one cigarette at a time
   D. Carrying a scepter

Learning Dave is 80-90% back.
They had to saw that bullsh#t
off my head.

CHAPTER 14

NEGOTIATION:

LET'S F#CK EACH OTHER OVER

Negotiation is like getting high and trying to find a cat: you'll find lots of cats that aren't lost. And you won't be sure; you'll keep bringing cats to the human mommy, saying, "Is this her? Is this Cleo?" And she'll say, "Nope." Now those cats that you "found" are lost because you brought them back. And you're like, "Fuuuuuuuck!"

—WARREN DALE BUFFETT

NEGOTIATION IS THE PROCESS BY WHICH two or more parties reach an agreement of how they are going to f#ck each other over. Negotiations are happening all the time, formally and informally, throughout the business world, and amazingly, technique is *everything*.

RULE #1: KNOW YOUR SITUATION

Know what you want, know what the "least" you'll settle for is, and know what will happen if negotiations fail. This last one is key to any negotiation; it's your **Best Alternative to Negotiated Agreement (BATNA).** This is your "best-case scenario" if negotiations are *not* successful. How does it look? If it's good (you're still selling eight million pygmy horses a week), you have great leverage, because you can always walk away from the negotiation room, but if it's bad, even Darth Vader they could literally ride around like a pony in there.

RULE #2: *THERE IS NO RULE NUMBER TWO*

Get it?

Knowing your situation is everything. On this last round,
our BATNA was going out to the grain silo and blowing the whole
team up, so we were happy to take it in the boo-boo.
—Keith V., Guinness World Record Holder, elbow coin-catch

Once you know your situation, how do you get what you want? Through these concepts and techniques:

Designate a walk-away point: Pick the price or term at which you would be willing to leave the negotiation.

Pick a walk-*around* point: This would be the price that makes you get up, walk around, stretch, maybe cut one . . .

Also know your *BAFGHGOH*: This is your Best Alternative which is F#cking Going Home and Getting Out of Here. Clearing your mind with medical marijuana.

ZEN-O-NOMICS

"How can we maximize profits?" the assistant asks the old wise CEO.

"Worry about profit only once we have paid our costs," he replies.

"I never told you this," says the assistant, "but we have the same mom."

Next, **apply pressure.** Tell them that you only have so much time to complete the negotiation (e.g., because you have to help Linda "pretty soon" because her van has bedbugs).

Use **ultimatums.** Draw a line in the sand (e.g., "If you don't do X, we will Y our brains out.").

Now **make them say "yes" seven times:** the Japanese discovered that a person can be put into a positive frame of mind by saying "yes." They realized also that seven was the magic number of repetitions that put a person into a compliant state. When negotiating, get the other side to do this, and you are in the power position. Here's one of the classic ways:

YOU: Knock knock.

THEM: Who's there?

YOU: Yes, yes, yes, yes, yes, yes, yes.

THEM: Yes, yes, yes, yes, yes, yes, yes who?

YOU: SIGN THE F#CKIN' PAPER.

And another oldie:

YOU: Come on, Jerry. Haven't we always been great clients?

THEM: Yes, you have.

YOU: What?

THEM: I said, "yes, you have."

YOU: What? [You've already got two yeses! Do this five more times!]

Finally, **change negotiators.** This is old-school tactics. Let them get right to the point of agreement, then say, "Great, I just hope we can get Dan to sign off on it. God he's tough."

You

Better yet, *you* step out and change into a costume: stumbling out of the Porta-Potty with a pigsticker and a Fu Manchu is a great way to make "Dan" into the scary reality that is *now*. (BTW: **Do not wear any of the following costumes during high-level business negotiations:** Rum Tum Tugger from *Cats*, E.T., "Sexy" Zombie, or R2-D2.)

And remember, never let them see you sweat. You've heard this before because it is true. You must project confidence: head still, eyes straight, voice in a lower register (do not squeal or scream), pelvis thrust tastefully forward, anus relaxed but ready, tongue firm, thighs flexed, heels flat on the floor, toes fanned in a "W," kneecaps aimed at a dot on the horizon, ball sack and breasts loose, thumbs toward ceiling, penis pointed at 7:15 o'clock, knuckles relaxed, and, when walking, arms swinging in the *opposite* direction of legs.

SOUNDS HARD, BUT IT'S FUN! READY TO GIVE IT A TRY?

The *Earn Your MBA on the Toilet* system is the only one to teach negotiation skills with live TalkingPage™ sessions. You will actually interact with the book program in real time! Those other f#ckers are going to look like cave-trash!

Ready? Let's go through your first live negotiation! The book's TalkingPage™ system will make a statement, and you will respond, out loud:

HI THERE! WELCOME TO YOUR LIVE NEGOTIATION SESSION. *[You talk here . . . just say "hi" or "hi, there" out loud.* OUT LOUD. *No one's gonna hear you. Do it. We can wait. You really need to do this or it won't work.]*

GOOD. LET'S SAY WE'RE NEGOTIATING TO BUY AN INVENTION FROM YOU. DO YOU HAVE ANY PRODUCT IDEAS, BY THE WAY? *[You]*

A "KID'S FOAM ZWAZZLE GUN." NICE. LET'S USE THAT. HOW DID YOU COME UP WITH THE IDEA? *[You -]*

WHOA, SLOW DOWN! JESUS. WOW, THAT'S A LONG STORY. WHAT DO YOU MEAN, YOU "POPPED YOUR BRAIN"? *[You]*

OUCH. DIDN'T KNOW UNICYCLES COULD EVEN GO THAT FAST. WHY WERE YOU *NAKED*? *[You -]*

AND WAS SHE? IMPRESSED? WAIT. WE SHOULD PRACTICE NEGOTIATION. ARE YOU GUYS TOGETHER STILL? YOU AND THIS GIRL? *[You]*

REALLY?! WHAT A BITCH . . . LET'S . . . WE SHOULD GET BACK TO THE—YOUR IDEA, THE ZWAZZLE TOY. HOW MUCH DO YOU WANT FOR THE IDEA? *[You -]*

I KNOW. THAT SUCKS. BUT WHAT YOU DID WAS PRETTY CRAZY. WE NEED TO FOCUS . . . DO YOU HAVE AN ASKING PRICE FOR THE TOY ZWAZZLE WIDGET THING? *[You -]*

LET IT OUT. TEARS ARE GOOD. TEARS ARE GOOD. *[You]*

SOUNDS LIKE SOMEONE IS KNOCKING ON THE BATHROOM DOOR. *[You -]*

I HEAR YOU. YOU'LL GET ANOTHER UNICYC—I THINK SOMEONE IS BUSTING DOWN THE DOOR. *[You]*

WE'RE GONNA BUTT OUT HERE. LOOKS LIKE YOU AND YOUR GRANDPARENTS HAVE SOME THINGS TO WORK OUT. GOOD JOB, BY THE WAY!

END OF SESSION

Excellent work!

When you're ready, **go back up to the top and DO IT AGAIN.** Remember, Henry Ford did everything *fifty times*. Practice makes perfect!

POP QUIZ!

1. In which major business negotiations were the following statements made?

    A.   "Uh huh, exactly."

    B.   "Hey Bob. Bob. Time to wake up. Bob."

    C.   "We are interested, but he's got to call us first, on a telephone."

    D.   "Aaachoo-motherf#cker!-choowoo!"

    E.   "What is dis, man? Dis is da bullshitting, man, okay?"

    i.   Bellcom East hostile takeover

    ii.   Citbankz purchase of Goldburg Howell Partners

    iii.   PizzaPoppa buyout by Trans Macaroni

    iv.   Banks a'Lot/Halloween Store Merger

    v.   Time Warner–AOL

2. The "BATNA" is:

    A.   Robin the Boy Wonder's partner

    B.   Important to get right THE FIRST TIME

    C.   Best Alternative To . . . 'Nother Word Right Here

    D.   Blow It Out Your Nana

3. When negotiating with naked people:

    A.   Get out of there.

    B.   Imagine them dressed.

    C.   Never look at their birdy. That's what they want.

    D.   Don't look like you're trying to smell them.

4. In a negotiation, an *experienced* mediator would:

    A.   Toss you around like a Beanie Boyby™

    B.   Be gentle yet screaming

    C.   Lick your neck and hair

    D.   Get everything of yours

CHAPTER 15

RULE-BASED BUSINESS PROCESS MODELING

YOU'RE PSYCHED! Why? 'Cause "rule-based business process modeling" isn't a real topic—we made it up! This is the "hangout" chapter—you can just hang out!

Think of this as your first Executive Business Lounge. A taste of the high life! And since it's not even a real topic, you're not missing anything, and you *automatically* get a B− (we don't want to draw attention).

So enjoy; hang out. To everyone else, it'll look like you're reading the hardest chapter in the book!

And have we got a surprise for you: AN OPTICAL ILLUSION!!

WHOA!

So trippy. So amazing.

What else? How about, what word is this: UMPKINP?

Pumpkin. That's right.

Hmmm. Anything in the bathroom you could play with? Guessing you don't have a harmonica. Still, it's relaxing to not have the pressure of studying.

Hang on. Getting a call.

Oh, shit. It is a real topic. The rule-based thing. Supposedly it's really hot right now. Fuuuuuck!

You guys are gonna get creamed. Y'all poor things were just hanging out. You're gonna look like idiots. Rats.

Sorry.

POP QUIZ!

(We know you didn't have any time with the material; that's been taken into account.)

1. **What is the capital of Nevada?**

   A. Las Vegas
   B. Reno
   C. Nevada Town
   D. God, what *is* the capital of Nevada?

2. **A "marsupial" is a what?**

   A. A kangaroo
   B. A rat
   C. A "special" rat
   D. Has a pouch

3. **John Dillinger, the famous gangster, built what famous dam?**

   A. Hoover Dam
   B. Goddamn
   C. Goddamnit
   D. Twenty-inch penis

Solar's gonna be huge. Hey, so I've got my wife's kid, Trevor, this afternoon. Hope it's cool if he watches a DVD while we work?

BUSINESS AND COMPUTERS!

Perhaps no technological development will have a
greater impact on how we do business than modern
computing. Even in the last few years, computers
have undergone some groovy changes like these:

▶ Computers have gotten smaller and may
  someday be found in larger dwellings such as
  blimp hangars.
▶ Computers have gotten faster. MIT's "Deep
  Throat," a gymnasium-sized adding machine,
  can compute 2 miniflops per life-snazzle.
▶ Computers have gotten smarter: the checkers
  computer TK-421 beat checkers Grandmaster

Michael Mary David Richard two times before detonating.

Imagine a future where every computer is connected to a central common network, called the "World Wide Wazzle." You could send mail to a friend with the press of a button, bringing a friendly bisexual compu-mailman to your door, who would whisk the letter away to your friend's yurt! STRAIGHT INTO YOUR MOUTH! WOULD YOU LEAVE YOUR HOUSE THEN?! It's going to be exciting.

"Deep Throat": a computer that plays checkers all the time

So what are some ways in which we will see computers assisting how we do business?

- ▶ Accounting computers: Maybe! These would seem to be a pipe dream at this point.
- ▶ Business statistics: Even computers have limits.
- ▶ Stock market programs: No.
- ▶ A disco computer! Now this has promise! Don't know what this would be, but having a little fun with the guys here in the mimeo room. They call us the "beard crew" 'cause of our beards, and we like to smoke a lid now and then, but yeah. Disco computer, love it!

CHALLENGES

▶ There is no way to "click" anything or move the cursor around except with the arrow keys; also, there isn't really a way to see what you're doing (there's no TV part, it's just this little mini-typewriter) and, due to design issues, this will always be the case.

▶ Even as computers get much smaller, they will always be too wide for residential doorways, making "home computing" an impossibility even for those with French doors.

▶ There is also an inevitable point at which the computers will unite, enslave robotic production, and annihilate the human race. But this seems a small price to pay* given that most say it won't happen until the summer of 2013.

WHAT'S THAT THING?!

It's called an "ATM" . . .

---

* For sexy, swinging long-haired compu-mailmen banging at your door with lids of sticky *sinsemilla*? Let's *hope* computers are here to stay!

Believe it or not, an Automatic Banking Machine, or "ATM," is a *robot*. Yes it is. Ask any robot expert of any university, and he'll tell you the same thing; it's a robot. But unlike a robot from science fiction that mainly follows the other characters around, an ATM serves a very important function in modern society: dispensing money!

How does an ATM work? The answer is deceptively simple! You stick the card in its eye and money comes out of its mouth. Before ATMs, people had to go in the bank and speak to a "teller," someone who "tells you" how they can help you!

All modern ATMs are a combination of a calculator plus a little TV screen plus a money box. And, just like a computer, they are programmed! } I/o cancel-
int main(){

                                        Int base
min; my_array[5];

                        Got it?

Could a person be rich enough to have their own ATM? Not yet, but it certainly is possible!

BETCHA DIDN'T KNOW!

In the movie *When Harry Met Sally*, in the scene where there's a mermaid on the boat after they get back, you can just make out an ATM in the background (hint: it's near the ambulance).

POP QUIZ:

1. **A TV attached to the typing part of a computer:**
   A. Would tip over the computer
   B. Would just show you what you already know: what you're typing!
   C. Is mixing business and pleasure
   D. You still couldn't move the cursor, so what!

2. **Which is the code for business?**
   A. std::cout << "Hippy=X << printable << std::endl;
   B. my_array[i] = i * 2; {include own dolphin}372398
   C. for(int i = 0; I am a Karate Black Belt i < 5; i++)
   D. 20 Goto 10

3. **Computer "programmers":**
   A. Will be international sex symbols
   B. Will literally be treated like minotaurs
   C. Will be Invincible Masters of the World Wide Wazzle
   D. Will earn $80 a pound for their sperm

A boat maker's business suffers when a drought hits the area, so he starts making submarines and drinking heavily. And then he gets fat and the rains come again, but he's not really into it anymore.

CHAPTER 17

INTERNATIONAL AND MULTIGLOBAL BUSINESS:
WHÅT YOÜ NEÉD TO KNØW

IN JAPAN, LIQUIDS ARE SLURPED, not sucked or swallowed. If you are in Tokyo and you are brought a bowl of a hot liquid and no utensils, begin to slurp it and then gently let the warm broth cascade out of your mouth and down on to your Dockers™ like a salty brown waterfall. AVOID EYE CONTACT FOR A BIT, then go in for another slurp. It's okay to groan.

If a **European** businessman shows you his or her dick, he's offering you gum. Just giggle or give a double thumbs-up. DON'T TAKE THE GUM—IT'S REALLY A DICK!

China believes that lead is a vitamin. Don't take vitamins there or lick the toys or the vitamins.

In **South America,** it is considered good luck to win the lottery.

If your hosts at a business dinner bring out a mystery meat and some sort of scoreboard, you're in **Mongolia.** They don't have business there; GET OUT!

Don't talk about leprechauns in **Africa. They have no framework for understanding that.**

The Canadians have over 400 different words for "anal sex."

BETCHA DIDN'T KNOW

"Emerging markets" are countries that have no buildings. If you visited one, you might actually think that you were at a giant farmers' market!

LEARN THESE HELPFUL PHRASES IN THE INTERNATIONAL LANGUAGE OF BUSINESS, FRENCH:

Are we taking you over? Or are you taking us over?	Belaba mo deedo? O Belaba mo doodee?
What happens now?	Du papa noc a niktu?
Are there toilets in this land?	Palapa lapa hey?
We like how you guys think.	Gicky.
We agree to your terms.	Pweeeeeeeeee!

Or . . . using International Business Sign, communicate with foreign partners quickly and efficiently.

Know the signs on the next page by heart.

A car salesman tells a man and woman that he has some models that may be "more in your price range." The man says, "I should put on a bee costume and sting everybody in this place."

"We accept your terms."

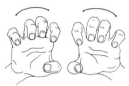

"We'll pay you one million dollars for that robot."

"Sorry. We thought he was a robot."

"THERE'S A PIECE OF BREAD IN THE TOILET!"

"Gentlemen: I wanna off myself."

"Fifty dollars for that ham, John? Are you crazy? That's not worth fifty dollars. We only want one ham."

"Your kilt is shredding."

"Does your culture have a hell?"

LAMINATE! LAMINATE! LAMINATE!

MULTIGLOBALISM: BUSINESS BETWEEN WORLDS

Assuming that this book will be used for the next several hundred years, it's very likely that you, the reader, live in a time when space travel is common. Mars in particular, we hope, supports hundreds of "life pods" each with a crew of four: a black, a white, a gay, and a magician.

Thus, business between planets *will* be a reality if it isn't already. First *between humans* on different planets and then between humans and Grays, Reptilians, and Annunaki.

Much of what you already have learned will be relevant to multiglobal business, and some will just be common sense:

1. **Know who you're doing business with:** The Japanese might expect gifts, but give them to the Annunaki and you might be asking for a THOROUGH probing.

2. **Dress the part:** A spacesuit is a safe, snazzy backup unless you know what kind of slimy kelp-dress-like thing they're draping over their hideous selves tonight.

3. **Be respectful:** Alien cultures will be different and may include things we find repugnant here: yogurt, "traditional music," facial hair. Pretend to embrace them. Save the snark for the quad-pod.

4. **Be cautious. Adjust:** These beings may be much more advanced and powerful than you. For example, if you've got Grays on a five-year ARM and they blow off payments, think about restructuring. Evictions can get messy when your tenants can spray acid out of their "noses."

5. **Get a good contract lawyer:** "ปอเปี๊ยะทอด," the Arcturian word for "supervisor," also means "eternal husband."

Doing business with the Annunaki

CHAPTER 18

THE STOCK MARKET:
LAS VEGAS FOR LOSERS

IN 1601 A DUTCHMAN NAMED PJOTER COCKALOFEN planted a buttonwood tree at the south end of Wall Street in Lower Manhattan . . .

Pjoter lost his mind, but the tree grew and became a meeting place for traders—men who would buy and sell shares in business ventures. It soon came to be known as the "**Cockalofen Buttonwood Exchange**," a name it proudly carries to this day (though some lazy assh#les call it the New York Stock Exchange).

While the **Cockalofen Buttonwood Exchange** is the world's *most important* stock market, it is now just one of many markets around the world where stocks, bonds, commodities, precious metals, and mutual funds are bought, sold, and traded.

"WAAAAAHHHH! I DON'T UNDERSTAND!!!!"

F#ck you. Chill out:

STOCKS A stock is a certificate of ownership of a tiny fraction of a publicly owned company. Imagine that Microsoft Inc. were a timeshare. The company would be the *condo*. The other "shareholders" would be Richard and Debby, Tom and Kimberley, and that other couple—the ones that Richard wrote "had f#cked all over the hot tub :(".

BONDS Instead of taking a loan from a bank, companies can take loans from the public by selling bonds. When you buy a bond, you are *lending* a tiny fraction of that total loan to the company, and you receive interest just like a bank would (the bond *yield*) until the money is paid back.

Bonds are for old people or others who do not have much longer on this planet: the terminally ill; those who live near geysers and volcanoes; the Annunaki.

COMMODITIES Tradable raw materials that fluctuate in value, like cotton. Yes, the same cotton that is used to make PANTIES!!! Calm down.

MUTUAL FUNDS A share of a bundle of assets. An investment bank puts together a mix of millions of stocks and bonds and continues to adjust that mix to try and maximize its return. It then sells fractional ownership of that huge bundle (and charges you for the service of "adjusting the mix"). If the bundle gains value, so will your tiny piece of that bundle.

If the "bundle" smells like a diaper . . . SELL!!!

STOCK PICKING

After you earn your MBA on the toilet, you might naturally expect your newfound expertise to give you a huge advantage in picking stocks.

Example of a stock market graph

The reality may be quite different. The renowned economist Burton Malkiel, who showed that stock price fluctuations are highly random, once wrote that "a **blindfolded monkey** throwing darts at a newspaper's financial pages could select a portfolio that would do just as well as one carefully selected by experts."

This is an absolutely *horrible* idea, starting with getting the blindfold on the monkey. Whether you're talking about a coffee can–sized squirrel monkey all the way up to a gibbon (which are big enough to drive a tractor) there's one thing monkeys *are* experts at, and that's biting and scratching the f#ck out of people.

Or worse: There was a real story in the newspaper about a monkey biting its owners' fingers off—*and they were actually trying to give it a birthday cake.* Imagine trying to put him in **a f#cking blindfold.**

And you still have to give him darts!

Malkiel suggested that the best strategy is to toss the darts on the floor and then run out and lock the door. Hopefully there's a window in the garage so you can see when he's done.

WARNING: He's going to do a lot more in there than just throw the darts: he's a monkey freely loose in a garage—armed—and without benefit of sight. Many monkeys in this situation will joke-practice their golf swing and then smash up your Miata with the 9 iron. Some will take a dump in your washing machine.

And there's more. Consider this: propane or fireworks in your shed? Maybe the situation has escalated? The feds surrounding your place? Langurs, lemurs, and macaques will **blow themselves up** rather than be taken alive.

Celebrating the MonkeyJobz.biz IPO

Is all that worth it? Just to beat the experts at the stock market? Ask Malkiel. In a lifetime of trying to perfect his monkey dart system, he lost every penny and saw the largest garage in Louisiana blown into a blinding cloud of newspaper, glass, and monkey meat.

Now let's take a closer look at some quiz!

POP QUIZ!

1. The stock market is:

A. A good way to learn about getting ruined

B. What it is

C. Low-hanging fruit

D. Pjoter Cockalofin's baby

2. The "Dow Jones" refers to:

A. A specific thing

B. An *unbeholdable and brain-destroying* thing

C. Dowmer P. Jones, III, founder of Beanie Boyby™

D. The ship that Donald Duck lost his mind on

3. The NASDAQ is:

A. The North American Stock Daq

B. The tribe that built the Teotixtlihuacan

C. A professional race car racing association

D. Similar to SCUBA diving

4. The New York Stock Exchange opens at:

A. 9:00 a.m.

B. 9:01 a.m.

C. Around 8, whenever the guy gets there with the key

D. It's open all night, with free drinks as long as you're buying stocks.

5. A stock market crash is _____

A. Loud! Wear earplugs.

B. Something that happens during a NASDAQ race

C. 100 percent fatal

D. Caused by a glitch in the *White Album*

KAREER KORNER!

An MBA is a very versatile degree. Not sure you want to work for a start-up, a bank, or an established company? Here are some alternative "business" careers where you can put your new MBA to great use!

CRUISE SHIP BLACKJACK DEALER X's and O's, queens, diamonds . . . poker is high-stakes "numbers fun" full time! As a blackjack dealer, you're in charge of a small team of people who are playing cards in front of you ON A MOVING SHIP. Must like working in groups. Perks: Better than accountant, the lowest.

VETERINARIAN Use your business brain to tend to sick animals around the globe as a veterinarian, an "animal doctor"! You'll be adding up the Benjamins every time you pump a shot into a lion or sea lion, and you'll be helping nature TO GET BETTER! Pluses: $$$$. Downer: Euthanizing movie stunt animals.

LOTTERY PROFESSIONAL Lottery is now big business, and as a lottery professional, you will drive around buying lottery tickets, scratchers, and Bingo Bonanzas until you win some kind of jackpot using your birthdate or someone's birthdate as the lucky number that you use over and over again. Set your own hours but leave plenty of time for smoking and drinking fun! Downsides: NONE! THIS IS FREE MONEY.

Q: When can I retire?

A: That's easy! Divide the number 80 by your high-school GPA and add 38. It works! Get out your calculator-watch and try it! (Age 58 if you had a perfect 4.0 . . . not till 78 if you pulled straight C's.)

JOCKEY Are you little? If so, you may be able to put that business mind of yours to use as a race-horsing rider. Jockeys are constantly using leadership, accounting, decision analysis, risk and operations, entrepreneurship, finance, pharmaceutical management, leadership and ethics, marketing, and media skills to coax that sweating brown beast to the podium. Gelding, foal, or filly, there's money in the pot for the tiny MBA with a lust for glory. Upside: Get to ride your own horse. Risks: None.

ENTREIOEPEOEUNEIOR Not to be confused with an "entrepreneur," these French "baking clowns" create fun and laughs in the kitchen, all while making a creme-stuffed form of brioche known as *gialupi*. Have you got the guts for it? You certainly have the degree! Before you decide: THEY ARE EUNUCHS. THAT'S A REQUIREMENT.

ACTOR/MOVIE SET CARPENTER Use your business acumen to build a real Jawa sandcrawler, then spend the evenings making love to actresses! That's the MBA life! CARPENTERS SHOULD ALWAYS WEAR A CONDOM. Remember that the pill will not prevent STDs.

REAL SUPERHERO People say the "real superheroes" are working moms, but that's bullshit. More and more people are making their own costumes and going out to fight crimes. Using your MBA, you could plan, execute, arrange, make a decision, make a mask and spandex suit, be a leader, and go out there and just go out with a bang.

TUNA FISHERMAN The most expensive tuna in the world just sold for $736,000! And you're sitting there at a desk?! Tell your boss to suck it, and start making some real money: tuna is the new private equity. Use your degree to chop that shit into chunks of purple cash.

BONUS ZONE!

BUSINESS MOVIE REVIEWS

THE PIANO This movie deals with the "business" of a very older, not-exactly-fat Irish man who is clammed up about his past and his helping of a very young piano player. The actual piano is brought there by boat, which gives you an idea of what you're in store for in this tearjerker. If you find yourself saying, **"What the f#ck is going on?!"** you should turn it off if you're alone, but if you're with someone, better keep your trap shut.

All in all, a weird, wild, and wonderful business movie.

RATING: A+++

B. J. AND THE BEAR (TV SHOW) Who needs to know more than that this lovable TV show was about a down-on-his-luck truck driver who has an animal that lives in the cab with him 24/7. It's not a bear. You never find out what it is. **It's a cute animal that is only named "Bear."** It's either a raccoon or something. But the man, little by little, works his way to the top with this animal companion, eventually becoming a priest of his own religion. SPOILER ALERT: He turns white and radiates light out of his head and "Bear" is transmogrified.

RATING: C+ [EXCELLENT]

AIRWOLF VS. BLUE THUNDER Let's have a little fun! This isn't exactly a review of a movie—**IT'S A BATTLE ROYALE** between the two greatest battle copters of all time! Which one wins? We say Blue Thunder because it has the backup of an elite police force, *and* Roy Scheider, who was a better pilot. What's your vote? (Hint, hint: It's Blue Thunder.)

AFTERWORD:
PRISON LIFE

AS YOU NEAR THE END of the second-most important journey of your life,* you need to face an important reality: YOU ARE GOING TO PRISON.

It's okay. You just need to know what you're doing . . .

THE BIG HOUSE

First, as a qualified MBA, you'll go to *federal* prison, and we think you're actually going to like what you see. They may not be the "country clubs" that they're made out to be, but they are a big step up from San Quentin, and you'll be walking in the footsteps of many great business leaders (including Carlo Ponzi himself).

---

* Nevada. When you got hit by the cone spreader.

SOME RULES TO LIVE BY WHILE YOU'RE THERE

TRY TO HOOK UP WITH OTHER MBAS OF YOUR RACE. Prisons are still heavily segregated, so even if your last group project was making dreamsicles with the Rainblo Coalition, check in with the shotcaller of your race before hanging out with others. If there is a gang war between MBAs, you'll fight for honor alongside your racial brothers, but it shouldn't be too bad because every single person in federal prison is a complete pussy.

IF THERE IS AN MBA GANG, JOIN IT. Gangs won't just fight for no reason, but if they do, you better belong to one of them or risk getting a slide rule in your assh#le. Here are some current prison gangs that are comprised mostly of MBAs or other business professionals:

- White Collar Brotherhood
- Ponzi Boyz
- The Oxley Sarbaños
- Account Choculaz (formerly Black Biznis Boy Posse)
- Lehman Bruthaz

NOTE: Do not offer business advice to the Nazi Lowriders, Black Guerrilla Family, or MS-13. They're more visual learners and will stab you with a toothbrush if you talk to them about business or anything else.

A TOOTHBRUSH CAN BE A WEAPON, A WEAPON AGAINST PLAQUE. USE IT. Avoid long horizontal strokes, which can damage enamel.

MAKE CONNECTIONS. Federal prison is a rich ecosystem of business talent, teeming with innovative thinkers, brilliant minds, and big-time douchebags. And you're one of them: you belong. Nervous? Pretend everyone's naked.

KNOW HOW TO DEAL WITH SCREWS. Prison guards and associated prison staff are known as "screws," and they can make your life a living hell. They must be treated with respect, but they can be bought. For drugs, cell phones, or weapons, be prepared to give points on the guard's mortgage or stock tips. Show them a picture of your Miata—remember, prison guards are douchebags, too.

LEARN PRISON ECONOMICS. You are not allowed cash in prison, though you may have an account at the commissary where you can buy Dr. Pepper, instant coffee, Cup-a-Soup, packaged mackerel, and Forever Stamps. You will use these items to pay for everything from hand jobs to haircuts. Never trade down, or you're gonna be the creep with fifty Kit Kat bars.

KEEP YOUR COOL. Graduating from federal prison can be one of the most emotional moments of your life. Don't bawl like an assh#le. You're free now. Try and get the Miata back. See if your leather jacket is in storage. Find the right pair of sunglasses, and get back to what you do best: getting the money.

And You're D-D-D-Done!

BUT I WANTED A DIPLOMA, WAAAAAAHHHHH!

Shut up. Cool it.

"Real" diplomas are bullshit. Why? Again: you need to shut your mouth. They're bullshit because they just sit at home on your wall . . .

Until now. Turn the page.

Wearable Diploma

MBA

Use scissors to cut this out and then use them to cut your hair. It's graduation day!

Did ya' learn a lot? Huhn? You ready to be a big shot? Yeeeaaahh. You know what? It's not *what* ya' know, okay. It's... You're booksmart. That's what you are. What did you say? Oh, now Learning Dave can't have a couple of drinks on his step-mom's birthday? Well fuuuuck you and congratulations. Congratu-f#ckin-lations. You're an MB-f#ckin'-A. Be well, my brother. Peace out. F#ck you.